IoT Design Briefs

Cellular IoT Ecosystems
- Design Concepts -

Kersten Heins

Preface

The IoT universe is expanding. New cellular networks like NB-IoT and LTE-M are offering unlimited Internet connectivity for IoT devices. **Cellular IoT technology (CIoT)** is inspiring the industry to exploit new application areas for the Internet of Things. By nature, professionally managed networks in licensed frequency spectrum are offering **unrivaled reliability** for business-critical applications. Cellular network standards are complex, but **off-the-shelf IoT products** are supporting developers to convert IoT visions into reality - and to benefit seamlessly from LPWAN functional strengths, e.g., from **lowest power consumption** for battery-driven IoT devices or from **deep penetration** into buildings or for underground sensing.

Motivation for this book series

IoT ecosystems are complex creatures. For each new IoT application, project owners and developers are facing tons of technology options and design aspects which need to be considered for a successful roll-out. Instead of accumulating all relevant information into a single large handbook, *IoT Design Briefs* are addressing carefully selected groups of **design aspects for IoT ecosystems** – focusing on concepts and design tips for IoT endpoints, security, Internet connectivity, cloud services, identity management, etc. They have been written for technical-minded IoT fellows as well as for engineering professionals who are planning the design and deployment of a new IoT application. On top of this, each book of the series offers regularly revised **technology updates and competitive comparisons.**

IoT Design Briefs provide qualified and meaningful information. Each *IoT Design Brief* has a focused scope and compact size – offered at a reasonable price.

About this book

This book is focusing on **top-level design aspects for of cellular IoT ecosystems (CIoT)** which are based on cellular mobile networks for Internet access and transmission of IoT data. It explains fundamentals and provides guidance how to build a decent CIoT ecosystem in short time.

Chapter 1 is titled "Introduction" and provides an overview about IoT use cases and typical IoT applications and target markets. Then, it introduces the structure and major building blocks of a generic IoT ecosystem

Chapter 2 is called "Cellular IoT (CIoT)". It explains the special characteristics of cellular networks, which IoT use cases are predestinated for NB-IoT or LTE-M. It also outlines how to leverage CIoT strengths for best results.

Chapter 3 is called "Building Blocks for a CIoT Ecosystem". It focuses on CIoT devices and provides an overview of required design ingredients. It explains how standard products, i.e., hardware components, software stacks, security elements and cloud services are providing an efficient design approach for reliable IoT applications.

Finally, a comprehensive **Glossary** provides explanations of frequently used technical terms and acronyms related to the Internet of Things and cellular network technology.

Last update: Jan 26, 2023 (V1.31)

Note: This is the first book of the *IoT Design Brief* book series. Book 2 has already been published and deals with network interfaces for CIoT devices. Book 3 will explain how to use the popular Raspberry Pi platform for CIoT studies and professional evaluations. Book 4 will deal with the IoT legal framework.

About the Author

Kersten Heins is a passionate technical consultant and content creator for IoT ecosystems, focusing on device design and embedded security (see www.iot-chips.com). After his graduation in Munich/Germany he spent 30 years in the industrial computing, semiconductor, and smartcard industry as a design engineer and in various marketing positions [1].

Besides various publications in blogs and newsletters, he wrote these books:
- "NB-IoT Use Cases and Devices - Design Guide", Dec. 2021, Springer International Publishing, ISBN: 978-3-030-84972-6 (Hardcover Book), ISBN: 978-3-030-84972-6 (Softcover Book), ISBN: 978-3-030-84975-7 (eBook)
- "Trusted Cellular IoT Devices", Jan. 2023, Springer International Publishing, ISBN: 978-3-031-19662-1 (Hardcover Book) and 978-3-031-19663-8 (eBook)
- "Cellular IoT Devices - Network Interfaces", Jan 2023, *IoT Design Briefs* book series (Book 2), self-published, ISBN: 9798374755350 (Paperback Book)

---

[1] Full profile, cv and list of publications is available at http://www.iot-chips.com/

Table of Contents

1 Introduction

The "Internet of Things" (IoT) is entering our everyday lives – either at work or at home or in public environments. We are dealing with smart devices which are connected to the Internet and delivering services which is either convenient for the IoT user or saves operational cost. The IoT approach is based on the idea that applications work automatically with remote controlled sensors and actuators – and without any human interaction.

Commercial expectations are high, and world-wide IoT industry and service providers are enthusiastic about forecasted market numbers and corresponding demand for billions of IoT devices. IoT success is fueled by a pervasive 24/7 Internet coverage while data transmission cost is continuously decreasing. IoT is following the concept of "edge computing", i.e., it manages end devices at remote locations to monitor and preprocess local data and perform local actions. While the remote IoT device performs autonomously most of the time, it is connected to the Internet and supervised by a central IoT application through the Internet. This way, simple "things" become smart IoT devices.

1.1 IoT Application Scope

As a matter of fact, IoT is an umbrella term for an endless list of target applications. Most of them are monitoring and analyzing conditions, aiming at an improved process efficiency resp. reduction of operational cost esp. for industrial or business-to-business (B2) use cases. Other IoT applications are helping to make everyday tasks more convenient and to improve quality of life. Many new IoT services and applications will affect our daily lives - either directly or indirectly. As a consequence, deployment of IoT applications concerns all of us and increasingly attracts public interest and also governmental attention.

"IoT" stands for an approach how to **improve existing use cases**. For example, a smart meter in households is able to determine individual power consumption, transmit is to the supplier who converts this data into a bill – automatically. Instead of manual data acquisition by service staff who has to visit each consumer regularly, smart meters are allowing access to consumption data at any time. This use case shows how the IoT approach can reduce cost and significantly increase process efficiency. There are many examples how the IoT is replacing traditional processes over time. This journey has just started.

But IoT also enables **new use cases** which have not been feasible so far. The IoT success story is driven by technology as well by the extending coverage of low-power wireless networks at continuously decreasing usage fees. This evolution, for example, enables tracking applications for mobile valuables via cellular or satellite-based IoT networks. Today, in combination with GPS/GNSS positioning you can locate a moving or movable object at any place of the world. Altogether, these advances are inspiring the industry to create new IoT services and products.

1.1.1 Industrial and Consumer IoT Markets

IoT is an approach, rather than an application or a group of applications. In general, IoT applications cannot easily be used for **IoT market categorization** because similar functions are used for different use cases. For example, predictive maintenance is a useful IoT application for industrial production sites and as well for transportation vehicles or for smart grids. Or, for example, surveillance of rooms or places is relevant for museums as well as for private premises or public train stations. A wearable fitness tracker is providing heart rate data to its owner in an effort to monitor and improve his training progress, but similar measurement of vital body data also works for eHealth scenarios where IoT data is feeding a remote medical service.

According to market researcher IoT Analytics[2], these are the top IoT applications areas and their global market share:

1. Manufacturing / Industrial – 22%
2. Transportation / Mobility – 15%
3. Energy – 14%
4. Retail – 12%
5. Cities – 12%
6. Healthcare – 9%
7. Supply Chain - 7%
8. Agriculture – 4%
9. Buildings – 3%
10. Other – 3%

In fact, IoT services are addressing different type of customers, i.e., consumers, patients, retail customers, service providers, manufacturers, or public institutions. Consequently, this differentiation can be used for further differentiation by looking at addressed **end user** roles, i.e., if a particular IoT service is addressing a **private or a professional** use case. Who will be using the offered IoT product? This categorization makes sense because each of these user groups are looking at (IoT-) products in a different way. Customer expectations differ so that providers of IoT services and devices will have to adjust product requirements accordingly. The term **"Industrial IoT (IIoT)"** is referring to professional IoT applications aiming at processes which are part of a business organization incl. manufacturing, logistics, deployment, maintenance, sales/marketing, etc. In general, IIoT is aiming at improvements in productivity and efficiency as well as other

---

[2] https://iot-analytics.com/top-10-iot-applications-in-2020

economic benefits[3]. In fact, IIoT is a so-called **business-to-business ("B2B")** scenario with an IoT provider supplying required components or a complete solution to an industrial user, i.e., a company.

On the other hand, non-IIoT applications are consumer applications addressing private end users. This is a **business-to-consumer ("B2C")** business model which is (at least) requiring a different marketing/sales approach by the IoT solution provider. The fundamental difference between B2B and B2C is that in B2C scenarios a business representative of the IoT provider (typically: a retailer) is selling a ready-to-use IoT product to a consumer, whereas in B2B we have professional staff of both sides.

Due to the nature of addressed use cases, consumer IoT products enjoy increased public visibility whereas only industrial insiders will be aware of typical IIoT processes, e.g., used in production sites warehouses of manufacturing companies. But the term "IIoT" is also used for other industrial tasks, not just for smart logistics or networked automation in manufacturing or predictive maintenance of production equipment. Instead, IIoT solutions are aiming also at industrial processes which are not related to manufacturing of goods, e.g., for remote healthcare services or retailing or energy distribution or farming applications[4]. B2B customers of IIoT solutions are hardware manufacturers as well as farmers, hospitals, energy suppliers, facility managers, car rental services and any other company interested in IoT approaches for professional use.

In addition to B2B and B2C scenarios, we have the **public sector**, which is managed or supervised by governmental authorities, e.g., garbage collection or the energy smart grid. For this kind of IoT products (for IIoT as well as non-IIoT usage),

---

[3] Boyes, Hugh; Hallaq, Bil; Cunningham, Joe; Watson, Tim (October 2018). The industrial internet of things (IIoT): An analysis framework" Computers in Industry. 101: 1–12.

[4] Gilchrist, A. (2016). *Industry 4. 0 : The industrial internet of things.* Apress L. P.

governmental parties might not buy themselves, but will kick off markets, specify products and related infrastructure for deployment, etc. Examples are smart meters or road tolling units or tachographs for vehicles which are either B2B or B2C IoT products but might not follow business B2B or B2C characteristics because of governmental regulations. Legal obligations also apply to other IoT products, esp. whenever an IoT service is addressing consumer markets. In particular, national governments have started to have an eye on privacy protection, so they are putting **cybersecurity laws** in place in an effort to protect citizen interests. Some IoT providers are not aware (yet), but each of them will have to pay extra attention to follow these rules in order to avoid legal consequences.

Figure 1 is illustrating typical IoT application areas and indicating how they are categorized as B2B, B2C and governmental business models.

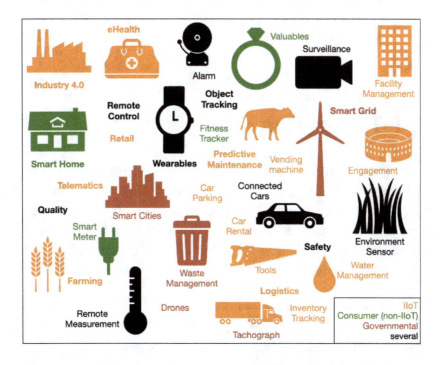

Figure 1: IoT Application Areas

Typical **IIoT applications areas** are for the "Industry 4.0" sector incl. smart factories, smart logistics, but are also covering retail or healthcare markets as well as the agriculture segment. "Smart Cities" is a collective term for IIoT applications initiated by public authorities to improve urban quality of life (e.g., security) or efficiency of public processes (e.g., waste management), but governments will not buy, but might certify suppliers and products. Same applies to smart grids for utility supply which is under governmental supervision (esp. the deployment of smart meters).

Only few application areas are **consumer IoT markets**, but they are huge. For the time being, smart homes are the most relevant market for consumer IoT systems. According to research company Statista, the Smart Home market reached a global sale of 99.41 billion USD in 2021 and is expected to grow to a total of 182 billion U.S. USD in 2025[5]. Another growing consumer market is following the "Quantified Self" movement[6] including popular fitness trackers. This market is supposed to reach a global size of 35 billion USD in 2025 (2019: 20 billion USD)[7].

1.2 IoT Ecosystem

In general, an IoT application is monitoring **multiple remote locations** (usually a large number) by sensing local parameters or just detecting local events, e.g., presence of an object. For this purpose, an IoT application is working with **IoT devices** sending local IoT which are reflecting relevant aspects of an observed environment or equipment. Figure 2 is outlining an IoT system with

---

[5] https://www.statista.com/topics/2430/smart-homes/

[6] https://quantifiedself.com

[7] https://www.marketstudyreport.com/reports/global-fitness-tracker-market-2020-by-manufacturers-regions-type-and-application-forecast-to-2025

just one sample IoT device. Raw IoT data set is being transmitted to a **central IoT application server** which is consolidating all IoT data streams received from connected IoT devices. On server side (or a cloud service), further data analysis and application-specific data processing will be performed and might result in actions to be performed locally ("remote control").

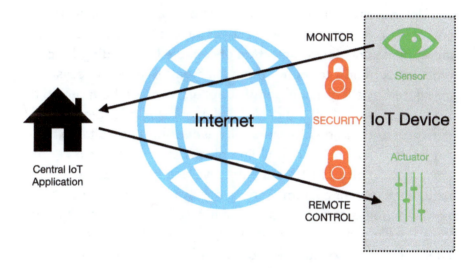

Figure 2: IoT Ecosystem

In short, an **IoT ecosystem** is formed from a set of elements which can be categorized like this:
1. Sensors and actuators and embedded application (device)
2. Network connectivity (communication channel)
3. Central application and data analytics (cloud software and services)
4. Security

IoT security measures provide protection against attacks and accidental misuse of an IoT application. Very often, an IoT application is competing against use cases which are attended or supervised by human operators. As such, it might qualify as an efficient alternative, if appropriate **IoT security** means have been implemented in an effort to ensure a trustworthy and reliable IoT application with remote frontend devices which are typically unattended. In general, IoT security affects all elements of the ecosystem, i.e., the device, the communication channel and cloud-based software. As a system concept, IoT Security has to be tailored to each use case.

Unfortunately, there is no standard ecosystem or platform for all kind of IoT use cases. Instead, each IoT project requires a business- and **application-specific selection of suitable IoT building blocks** and a concept how to merge them. Elements of an IoT ecosystem are offered by a large number of suppliers, each of them providing products or services in their area(s) of expertise. IoT project managers and business owners will have to short-list suitable candidates for all relevant building blocks of a suitable IoT ecosystem. In order to offer an attractive one-stop-shopping experience to their customer, many hardware suppliers are bundling their core products (e.g., a network interface module) with corresponding cloud-based services, e.g., an IoT device management tool or subscription plans for network connectivity.

On top of collaboration with suitable business partners, IoT projects will have to meet governmental obligations which are often aiming at personal data protection or fraud prevention. In addition, some IoT products will have to proof compliance with dedicated security regulations for specific target markets, esp. for national projects of public interest, e.g., tachographs for vehicles.

2 Cellular IoT (CIoT)

This issue of our *IoT Design Brief* book series is focusing on the design of cellular IoT (CIoT) ecosystems which using mobile networks for Internet connection of IoT devices. Cellular networks are standardized and offer reliable IoT connectivity almost everywhere on this planet.

Choice of network technology does not change the fundamental structure of an IoT ecosystem (refer to Figure 2), but cellular networks have special characteristics which are explained in this section. Based on the fact that cellular networks are owned by external service providers, cell structure and network coverage is fixed. Selection of a suitable provider is a key aspect. On top of this, a tailored adjustment of key network parameters requires carefully designed CIoT endpoint devices.

2.1 Cellular IoT Ecosystem and Endpoints

All local activities are handled by smart IoT devices. An IoT device is a dedicated embedded system which is acting on behalf of the IoT application and located close to data sources of interest, i.e., at the far end of an IoT application ("edge computing"). An IoT device is a remote-controlled MCU-based system which is running independently and does not require any local human interaction. Very often, the device does not offer any local user interface at all. Instead, the IoT device is a managed by embedded **IoT application** which is working in cooperation with the central IoT application, i.e., the overall IoT application is separated into a **local part** running on the IoT device and a **central part**.

Figure 2 is illustrating the main functional elements of an IoT device. The embedded IoT software is mainly responsible for hardware control and typically does not require much computing power, i.e., a simple 1-dollar microcontroller can handle it. This part of the IoT application is fixed and has been stored permanently in a non-volatile memory during production, therefor also called **IoT firmware**. The IoT firmware starts after right after a IoT device has been powered up or after a device reset and works offline, but supervised and interruptible by the IoT server, if needed. Optionally and if required, it can also be updated by the IoT server via network (FOTA = firmware-over-the-air). The device firmware determines the hardware flow, i.e., order and type of local actions, and manages other device components via dedicated interfaces (e.g., GPIO pins or serial I^2C or UART interfaces accordingly. For this purpose, each local peripheral interaction needs to be converted into dedicated I/O control and data commands to be submitted according to the interface protocol specifications. The IoT firmware has to communicate with the **network interface** module and interact with peripheral IoT **sensors and actuators**. Besides these components for remote sensing and control, Internet connectivity is another fundamental IoT requirement. The network interface is a key element and one of the most complex building blocks of the IoT device design. Usually, it is implemented as a dedicated network subsystem (network interface module) with an integrated MCU, memory, RF-section incl. antenna interface and SIM card interface. Network interface modules are quite expensive (around 10 USD or more), but they handle lower network layers independently and offer a high-level API which allows the local IoT firmware to delegate adjustment of network parameters, establish connections and handle communication sessions. In addition, Internet sockets and protocols as well as security functions are providing significant added value to the core function of the network interface.

The local IoT application can also perform simple calculations and take basic decisions, e.g., if a certain pre-defined threshold has been exceeded and requires submitting an alert to the central IoT application (example: local ambient temperature is exceeding a certain, predefined range).

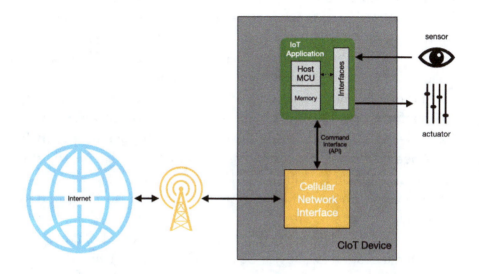

Figure 3: Block diagram of a cellular IoT device

A fundamental truth is that different IoT applications are following different objectives. So, each IoT device will be looking for different local conditions and require different edge computing capabilities. In fact, each IoT application requires tailored sensors and actuators, a suitable microcontroller plus memory, matching connectivity parameters (range, latency, data rate, etc.) and additional functional elements or services. As a consequence, there is **no off-the-shelf general-purpose IoT device** available on the market. For IoT application owners it would be beneficial to use a configurable standard IoT platform offering all required features and configure according to custom requirements. This approach would be able to reduce own development activities and increase time-to-market. But this approach would be too expensive because, each customer would have to pay for redundant components (e.g., a temperature sensor) or functions (e.g., battery management) which are not required for every IoT application. Consequently, at least for large-scale IoT installations, unit price limitations will justify development of a tailored **custom IoT device with optimized characteristics**. Fortunately, designers can benefit from standard lower-granularity IoT functional elements such as network interface modules, sensors, antennas, etc. incl. software building package and associated high-level APIs. This subject will be explained later in chapter "IoT Design with off-the-shelf elements".

From a technical perspective, it is possible to set up a **generic IoT platform** which is able to address different IoT use cases. For example, single-board computer systems like popular Raspberry Pi have been designed to offer ultimate flexibility and can be adjusted for any application-specific need. Hardware extensions in combination with a suitable software configuration and embedded application programs are allowing a customer to put a complete IoT device in place with lowest effort and in a short period of time. Although a custom IoT device based on Raspberry Pi would be too expensive for a large-scale commercial IoT deployment, this approach makes perfect sense for IoT feasibility studies, evaluation of components or as a mock-up, e.g., for demonstration purposes

Note: Mockups for cellular IoT devices and an LTE-M/NB-IoT network tester based on Raspberry Pi will be handled in an extra *IoT Design Brief* called "CIoT with Raspberry Pi".

2.2 Cellular vs. other IoT networks

Usually, IoT connectivity requirements can be handled by standard network technologies available on the market. For some IoT target environments (e.g., for production facilities), fixed networks can be used, but for most IoT deployments use of a wireless network is more efficient. By nature, a wireless network offers flexible connectivity to arbitrary device locations which are within reach of a network access point. For mobile applications resp. use cases with moving resp. movable IoT devices, fixed networks cannot be used anyway. But even for stationary IoT devices, an **external wireless option** might be useful in addition to an existing network infrastructure. This is particularly beneficial whenever the target deployment area might be difficult to control by the IoT service provider, e.g., a local area network (LAN) in a private site or an office building. In this case, the IoT device can be managed via wireless connection in a fully independent manner.

2.2.1 Wireless Network Technology Background

Wireless communication is based on transmission of **electromagnetic waves**. Electromagnetic waves are produced whenever electric charges are accelerated, i.e., whenever an electric field changes. This means that an alternating current flow through a wire will generate electromagnetic waves which are reflecting these alternations. The frequency of the waves created in this way equals the frequency of the alternating current. Generated waves are carried away from the current flow, i.e., the wire works as a transmission **antenna**. The inverse physical effect works as expected: if an electromagnetic wave strikes a wire, it induces an alternating current of the same frequency in the wire. This is how the receiving antennas of a radios or television sets work. An antenna is most efficient when its dimensions are equivalent to 1/4 wavelength of the waves emitted or received. Electromagnetic waves travel at light speed at $3,0 * 10^8$ m/s, i.e., at a frequency of 1 GHz a wave would have a length of $(3 * 10^8$ m/s$) / 10^9$ m/s $= 0,3$ m $= 30$ cm → the optimal antenna length would be 7,5 cm.

This fundamental physical phenomenon was originally used for analog data like voice or pictures but can also be used to transmit a digital data stream. For this purpose, the original payload data has to converted into a serial signal ("baseband") before it will be used to modulate a RF carrier frequency. Different wireless network technologies use different modulation techniques how to integrate both waveform sources. For example, a simple frequency modulation (FM) can encode data in a carrier wave by varying its frequency. For illustration purposes in Figure 4, the FM method is used to explain the operating principle how an electronic device converts digital data into a wireless transmission signal.

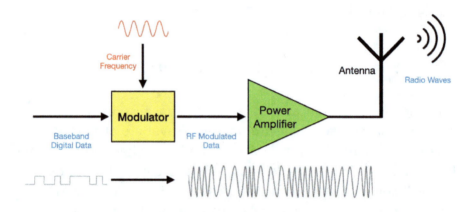

Figure 4: Operating Principle of Wireless Data Transmission

After modulation of the RF carrier, the integrated signal will be powered up in order to fuel the antenna. Typical carrier frequencies of 1...5 GHz used for wireless data communication standards travel in straight line, so both sender and receiver must be strictly aligned in **line-of-sight**. Waves will easily go through empty space or through insulating materials but cannot pass conducting materials. Concrete, with and without metal reinforcement, is one of the worst building materials for wireless signals to pass through. Instead, they will bounce back. But the signal will not lose energy while the carrier wave crosses plywood or drywalls. As a general physical rule, travelling radio waves at lower frequencies are less sensitive to obstacles, and they also resist bad weather conditions, but the power of low frequency waves decreases sharply as they cover long distance. High frequency radio waves have more power.

2.2.2 Wireless Network Options

Each commercial IoT project is based on its own business conditions, and some technical aspects might be fixed requirements. For example, if you follow an invitation to a public tender for a national smart meter project, used network technology and infrastructure will be predefined, i.e., not negotiable. But in most cases and from a technical point of view, various wireless technologies will be able to meet requirements of a specific IoT application, not just one. Figure 5 provides an overview of popular wireless technologies which might be used for IoT projects.

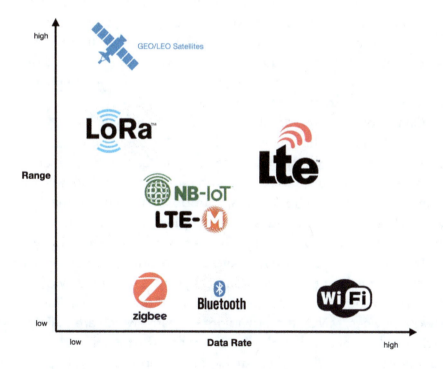

Figure 5: Wireless IoT Networks

Besides the range of a network, transmission speed (rata rate) is another major differentiator and an important parameter when comparing wireless technologies. illustrates these parameters for mentioned standards in a matrix overview. Max. network range leads to a common categorization of wireless technologies as Local Area Networks (LANs) like WiFi, Zigbee, Bluetooth or Wide Area Networks (WANs) like LTE and low-power WANs (LPWANs) like LoRa, NB-IoT and LTE-M.

Independent from technical characteristics, a fundamental difference is the applied **network service business model**, i.e., how a network is managed and how services are provided. Use of **licensed bands** are offered by external professionals as a fee-based service, typically by Mobile Network Operators (MNOs) which are also owning the network infrastructure. Access is based on a contract-based "subscription plan" specifying applicable fee per access, per message, per data volume, etc. In return, the user will get a stable and reliable network including cloud services for usage statistics, device management, etc. For use of unlicensed bands, these usage fees do not apply because the network is owned and managed by himself. In fact, the user has to purchase equipment and maintain the network infrastructure by own staff.

On top of this, a major difficulty of wireless networks in **unlicensed bands** is that many operational devices using the same channel in close proximity might interfere with each other, which can make the band unusable. Although regulations and technical means (e.g., frequency hopping) are supposed to mitigate this risk, by its nature a licensed band is potentially less noisy than an unlicensed band and potentially offers a higher level of reliability.

In light of increasing **privacy and data security** requirements for electronic equipment, proper authenticity and confidentiality of data transmission should be considered carefully. For use with cellular network devices, MNOs are providing SIM cards which are mainly used for subscription control but also act as a trust anchor (immutable device identity) for strong end-to-end security. Usually, fixed LANs offer lowest vulnerability, but for a secure short-range wireless network, ZigBee is a good choice. Bluetooth should be avoided; WiFi requires extra care to configure equipment properly.

Power consumption is a serious concern particularly for battery-driven endpoint devices which are supposed stay operational for a long time. Standard LTE network devices eat much more power than WiFi devices, but of them require frequent battery recharge during operation. As a general rule, for all wireless devices, the RF part of the device is dominating its power budget, even if limited to 100mW for data transmission. This is a problem for devices which must be online and available all the time. For a long battery life, an infrequent "pulled" and/or scheduled "push" data transfer scheme would be an advantage, if the target application allows for it. NB-IoT has been designed for these kind of operation modes.

Based on listed criteria, Table 1 provides an overview how wireless network technologies compare.

	Licensed (L) or unlicensed (U) frequency band	Transmission Speed (kbps)	Max. Range (m)	Topology	Power consumption (device)	Security
Bluetooth	U	1000	100	Mesh	low	poor
ZigBee	U	250	100	Mesh	low	good
WiFi (IEEE 802.11a), 5GHz	U	54000 +	150	Star	medium	ok
LoRaWAN	U	50	15k	Star	low	good
NB-IoT	L	250	15k	Star	very low	very good
LTE	L	10000	10k	Star	high	very good

Table 1: Wireless Network Comparison Chart

2.2.3 Cellular Wide-Area Networks (LPWANs)

Originally, this cellular network approach has been developed as GSM (= "Global System for Mobile Communications") technology for digital mobile phones – to be used across national borders. International cooperation work started 1982 in Europe, and first GSM networks were implemented from 1992 onwards. Over time, technical specification work moved from European ETSI to **3GPP** [8] (3GPP="Third Generation Partnership Project"). 3GPP is the global standardization organization behind the evolution and maintenance of GSM, UMTS, LTE and 5G cellular radio access technologies. 3GPP work is coordinated by regional organizations representing Europe, USA, China, Korea, Japan, and India. Since its start in 1998, 3GPP is publishing work items in **annual release cycles**. For example, Release 16 was issued in 2020. Each release contains a set of features providing functionality across GSM, UMTS, LTE and 5G and making sure that these technologies will coexist and interoperate.

3GPP cellular network standards in combination with governmental **spectrum auctions** are the foundation of a well-established **business model for cellular network operators** who are offering services to users of mobile phones incl. smartphones. These operators are called MNOs (MNO="Mobile Network Operator"). With more than 5 billion subscribers worldwide, this is an unparalleled success story and a win-win situation for MNOs as well as for network users. An industry organization called **GSM Association**[9] (short: "GSMA") represents the interests of worldwide MNO members - and besides the 3GPP website – a good starting point for potential users and other parties interested in cellular network technology.

Fundamentally, all 3GPP cellular networks are based on a large number of adjacent signal areas called **cells**. These cells join or

---

[8] https://www.3gpp.org
[9] https://www.gsma.com

overlap each other. Within each cell you will find a **base station** or **cell tower** which sends and receives data. Base stations are access points allowing user devices to connect to the MNO network. For IoT devices, a connected base station is acting as the entry point for Internet communication, i.e., to transmit IoT payload data or receive control information (see Figure 6). Each cell is covering a certain area providing wireless Internet access to user devices within reach.

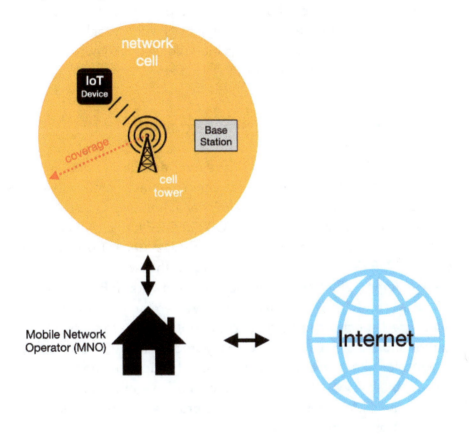

Figure 6: Cellular Internet Access

A cell tower is a platform where antennas and other hardware are being mounted. Physically, this could be a dedicated mast or a building. In general, cell range (or cell size) depends on used antenna and applied output power (which might be restricted/limited by regional law). In rural areas, a single network cell will be able to cover an area of up to 35 km. By nature, **cell coverage** area will be small in urban areas because high-frequency radio waves cannot easily pass building walls easily. On the other hand, high population in urban areas means a lot of users might request service at the same time. But each cell can handle a limited number of user connections only. This means that a new connection request would be rejected by a cell if its **capacity** is exhausted. This gap will be compensated by additional cells within reach of a user terminal, i.e. In high-demand areas multiple cells with overlapping cell ranges areas will be provided.

2.2.3.1 NB-IoT and LTE-M vs. LTE and 5G

Originally, cellular networks have not been designed to meet **IoT requirements** right from the beginning. In fact, some early IoT-usable features have been offered by cellular networks since 2nd generation. Until early 2015, GSM/GPRS/EDGE had been the main cellular technology of choice for serving wide-area IoT use cases. At this time, GPRS was a mature technology with low modem cost. But market demand for low-power wide area networks (LPWANs) was increasing and GPRS was challenged by alternate technologies in unlicensed spectrum like Sigfox, LoRa. Anticipating this new competition, 3GPP started a feasibility study called "Cellular system support for ultra-low complexity and low throughput Internet of Things" back in 2016. These efforts resulted in ambitious objectives for cellular IoT features in a post-GPRS era. Main goals for the specification of NB-IoT were:

1. improve cell **coverage** for rural areas and **penetration** of buildings down to ground level
2. reduce **device complexity and cost** in order enable massive IoT applications
3. network **latency** should not exceed 10 seconds

4. achieve high **capacity** for a massive number of IoT devices generating a small amount of data
5. minimize device **power consumption** to achieve 10 years lifetime of a 5Ah battery
6. **reuse existing LTE network** infrastructure and upgrade with new IoT features by software only.

Figure 7 is illustrating the objectives for NB-IoT.

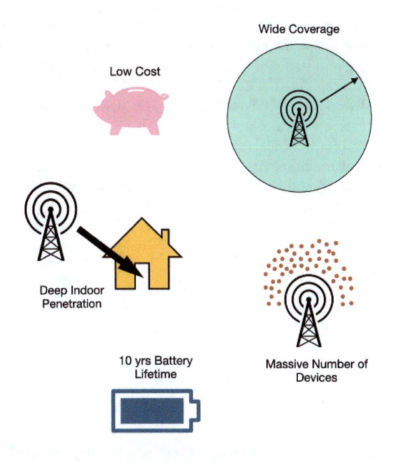

Figure 7: NB-IoT objectives

As a result of related standardization work and worldwide agreement, **NB-IoT** (= "Narrowband IoT") has been defined as an add-on to 4G/LTE in 3GPP Release 13. From now on, IoT connectivity became an integral part of cellular technology. Dedicated IoT network technologies NB-IoT and LTE-M have been specified a couple of years ago, and worldwide network deployment is growing continuously. According to market researcher Counterpoint, NB-IoT is the leading cellular IoT network today[10] - and still will be good after 5G will be widely deployed. Major driver for NB-IoT deployments is China. By the end of August 2022, the **number of IoT connections** in China had reached 1.698 billion, **surpassing the number of mobile phone users** for the first time[11]. LTE and standard LTE networks can be used for IoT purposes if high data rates are needed. Both LTE and 5G networks will offer lower network latency than NB-IoT and LTE-M, but still will fall behind in terms of low power consumption and indoor coverage. In general, all current cellular technologies can be used for IoT, but do not meet all requirements equally. Table 2 provides a rough overview of strengths and weaknesses of CIoT network options available today resp. soon to come.

---

[10] https://www.counterpointresearch.com/global-cellular-iot-module-forecast-2030/

[11] http://english.www.gov.cn/archive/statistics/202209/21/content_WS632af6ffc6d0a757729e0525.html

Requirement	LTE / 5G	LTE-M	NB-IoT
Data Rate	✓✓✓	✓✓	x
Network Latency	✓✓	✓	x
Indoor Coverage	✓	✓✓✓	✓✓✓✓
Battery Lifetime	x	✓✓✓	✓✓✓✓
Capacity	✓	✓	✓✓✓
Mobility	✓✓	✓✓	✓

Table 2: Cellular Standards – IoT Application Requirements

The cell capacity requirements target for NB-IoT in (for 3GPP Release 13) has been set to 40 devices per household which corresponds to 52.500 devices per cell or 60.680 devices per km². In combination with a high density of small cells in urban areas state-of-the-art cellular LPWAN network implementations will enable **massive connectivity**. In fact, a mobile phone or IoT device usually connects to the closest available base station, if not congested by other user devices. As an alternative, it may connect to the next available channel offered by another cell within reach. Figure 8 illustrates a typical scenario for an IoT device in need for a data connection to a cellular network. In this case, the IoT location in within reach of three different cells – operated by the same or by different MNOs.

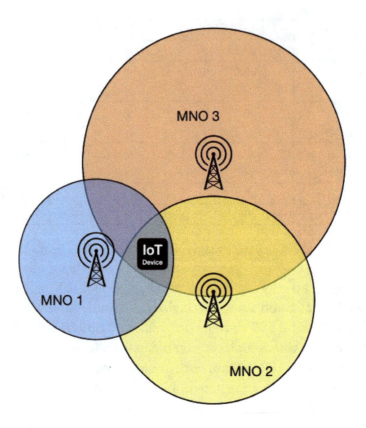

Figure 8: IoT device covered by multiple cells

Cellular low-power IoT (LPWAN) connectivity has two types: **Narrowband IoT (NB-IoT) and LTE-M**. Although both are based on LTE cellular standard, a major difference between the two is that NB-IoT has a smaller bandwidth than LTE-M, and thus offers a lower transmission power. In fact, its bandwidth is 10x smaller than that of Cat-M1. In general, cellular IoT offers excellent reliability and qualifies for mission critical applications. In addition, device operational lifetimes are longer as compared to unlicensed LPWAN. But when it comes to choosing between one of them, **NB-IoT** is often preferred because it addresses typical IoT applications at **lower cost vs. LTE-M**. Typical IoT applications (see next chapter "CIoT Use Cases") are **infrequently sending a small amount of data,**

e.g., meters or detectors. On the other hand, LTE-M offers mobility support and voice data transfer which is useful for transportation and tracking applications. As a rough indication, LTE-M could be a better choice for mobile applications, NB-IoT for indoor or stationary applications.

As explained, use of cellular IoT networks is not for free, i.e., usage fees and subscription plans apply. At first glance, they look expensive. Wi-Fi and other wireless networks in unlicensed spectrum appear as complimentary and a good deal. But this is only part of the story. More important for a reasonable competitive comparison is the so-called **"total cost of ownership (TCO)"** criteria which is calculated in completely different way for networks in **licensed vs. unlicensed frequency range**. A major differentiator is based on the fact that cellular network operators are independent service providers. They own the complete network infrastructure and will provide IoT connectivity essentially everywhere as a service. In contrast, an unlicensed connectivity infrastructure will be installed case-by-case at locations where IoT connectivity is needed for specific purpose, e.g., in office building or at home. These installations are usually owned by the user who will have to provide network access points, user management, secure operation, sufficient network capacity, etc. Dedicated maintenance staff must be hired to ensure service delivery, software updates, cloud interfaces, user support, etc. Related one-time investments and recurring operational cost are impacting TCO and should be calculated for a realistic and fair competitive comparison of licensed vs. unlicensed connectivity solutions.

Another good reason to consider using a cellular IoT network is **scalability** which is a critical requirement for massive IoT deployment scenarios. This means that used network must be able to handle a growing number of users or changing coverage conditions. For example, some countries have initiated **national rollouts of smart meters** in order to track power consumption in households. For this purpose, country-wide and robust coverage network coverage is mandatory because IoT devices might be located virtually everywhere and require reliable connectivity even under worst conditions, e.g., if installed in underground basements. For this kind of wide-area IoT projects in an unpredictable and uncontrollable environment, a cellular network offers significant advantages.

Another major benefit of a cellular IoT solution is that used network infrastructure is **always up-to-date** and future-proof. Cellular networks are based on **global** standards with very large industry support including manufacturers, network operators and service providers. **Long-term support and reliable service delivery** is quasi guaranteed because of billions of users all over the world are using it.

In general, each IoT project is aiming at different environments and facing different conditions at target locations. One of the key prerequisites for a successful IoT concept is a clear understanding of **requirements for deployment** of IoT devices. How many will be installed and where? In general, cellular network devices are easier to deploy because connectivity depends on network coverage only: if the IoT device is within reach of a network cell, Internet connectivity will work for this device. At first sight and for example, using an existing Wi-Fi network free-of-charge at point of deployment looks like a reasonable approach. But will it work, will local network coverage reach all locations and provided capacity guarantee for reliable service of all IoT devices? In fact, an existing network installation can help, if well-known and under control. In all other cases or in case of uncertainty resp. mission-critical IoT applications, use of cellular IoT networks should be considered – at least as a fallback option. If cellular network technology is used, no specific knowledge nor re-configuration of local IT network infrastructure (e.g., routers) will be necessary. This might be beneficial because installation of cellular IoT devices is **independent from existing local IT landscape**, if available.

Anyway, sales numbers provide evidence that NB-IoT is the leading cellular IoT technology, see Figure 9. As already mentioned, NB-IoT is forecasted to maintain its #1 position even after full deployment of 5G because 3GPP releases 13-15 are already matching high-volume CIoT applications with low-date rate requirements in a cost-efficient way, e.g., for remote metering or asset localization. Instead, later 3GPP release will focus on extension and improvement for different application areas.

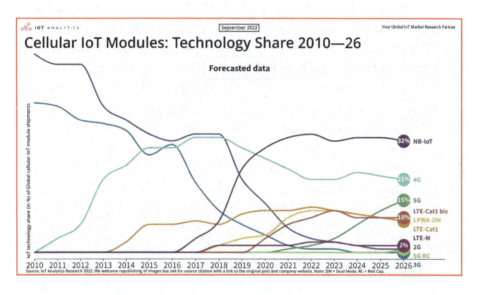

Figure 9: CIoT Market Share 2010-26 (Source: IoT Analytics [12])

2.2.3.2 Network Coverage and Service Providers

By nature, presence of a cell with sufficient coverage is crucial for CIoT connectivity. In fact, access to a cell will be granted only if the requesting user device has a valid business agreement with the **cell owner** is in place, a so-called subscription plan. So, for each

---

[12] https://iot-analytics.com/iot-modules/

cellular IoT project, selection of a suitable connectivity partner is a key ingredient for a successful rollout because all locations of an IoT device must be covered. GSMA coverage maps[13] plus further details provided by MNOs will be good starting points. In an effort to extend coverage of their networks into other geographic regions, many MNO have **roaming** agreements with other MNOs covering different regions in place.

In addition to traditional MNOs, so-called **"virtual" network operators (MVNOs)** are offering cellular network services which are based on business agreements with these network infrastructure owners (MNOs). Consequently, a MVNO might offer multiple access points – operated by different MNOs – for IoT devices at its particular deployment location (refer to Figure 8). This strategy extends the usable overall network coverage area.

3GPP network standards are ensuring interoperability of different implementations, but MNOs use different network configurations. Some of them are negotiable via user API (so-called AT commands), but some are fixed. For example, the so-called "inactivity timer" of a network which is managing an as-early-as-possible disconnection of the device is **not user-configurable**. Consequently, for an IoT deployment it is useful to check all of them, esp. if application-specific resp. optimized network parameters are required, e.g., to achieve lowest power consumption for battery-powered IoT devices.

Note: An LTE-M/NB-IoT network tester based on Raspberry Pi will be handled in an extra *IoT Design Brief* called "CIoT with Raspberry Pi". This vehicle allows users to perform local trials and studies.

---

[13] https://www.gsma.com/iot/deployment-map/

2.3 CIoT Use Cases and Applications

Typical IoT applications are monitoring local parameters at remote locations. IoT target markets and application areas have been outlined in chapter "IoT Application Scope", list of target business cases is endless. For some **mission-critical** IoT applications, use of a cellular network is recommended because an operator-managed cellular network in licensed spectrum offers ultimate reliability and sustainability for a moderate usage fee, esp. when only small amount of transmission data is required.

Besides that, LPWAN technology (incl. cellular LPWAN) is needed for **wide-area** applications requiring a network range of kilometers (refer to Table 1), i.e., for outdoor applications or for uncontrolled (urban) environments which do not allow to reduce distance between network access points and IoT sensors.

On top of that, NB-IoT has been designed for IoT applications with one of the following characteristics:

- battery powered IoT devices with ultra-long lifetime
- infrequent transmission of small data packets with low data rate (with relaxed latency requirements)
- large number of connected devices in same cell (high device density)
- deep indoor or underground penetration

2.3.1 Examples for real-world CIoT installations

Cellular LPWAN network capabilities match connectivity requirements of many IoT applications for industrial as well as for consumer markets. These network technologies will be first choice whenever high cell capacity or deep inhouse resp. underground penetration will be required, esp. in use cases requiring battery driven IoT endpoint devices. Not surprising, many NB-IoT deployments are aiming at Smart City, Smart Farming, Smart Home, Smart Grid, Retail or asset tracking applications.

Here is a selection of a few typical cellular LPWAN IoT products or deployments. Across all segments mentioned in earlier book section "Industrial and Consumer IoT Markets", these real-world examples are revealing the variety of CIoT target applications and the overall potential of LPWAN technologies like NB-IoT:

Digital Oilfield

In the past, Shell Nigeria was relying on a series of manual processes for wellhead monitoring and pipeline surveillance. Now, based on battery-driven IoT sensors, Shell is able to monitor installed oilfield infrastructure, prevent unscheduled maintenance and even solve detected issues remotely. This is increasing operational efficiency and safety – and saves cost[14].

IoT Robot checks retail store inventory

Making sure that shelves are always filled with the right item and marked at the correct price is crucial for retailers. These tasks must be repeated over and over, typically take several hours to complete, and tend to be very inaccurate when done by humans. As an alternative, company simbe offers an IoT solution which relies on an autonomous robot called "Tally"[15].

"Green" Olympics Stadium

A building automation system installed by company Honeywell turns a stadium in Beijing/China for more than 100000 athletes and visitors into an energy-efficient and safe site. More than 7500 controlled points, 769 sensors incl. 37 water valves and 106 air dampers have been used[16].

---

[14] https://www.ingenu.com/solutions/industries/digital-oilfield
[15] https://www.simberobotics.com
[16] https://inbuildingtech.com/venues/honeywell-smart-stadium/

Predictive Maintenance for ThyssenKrupp Elevators

IoT solution predicts maintenance issues before they occur, and empowers elevator engineers by flagging the need to replace components and systems before the end of their lifecycle[17].

Connected Sheep in Norway

Problem is that farmers gathering their animals face difficulties to find all of their animals. Network operator Telia Norway and a partner company equipped 1000 sheep with collars with NB-IoT tracking modules which are used to remotely track and monitor the animals[18].

Air Quality Index (AQI) Sensor

Company Libelium[19] is offering its Waspmote environmental IoT sensor in a robust waterproof IP65 enclosure with specific external sockets to connect the sensors, optional solar panel, etc. Several configurations are available incl. electro-chemical gas sensors providing extremely accurate ppm values and a high-end dust sensor.

Mouse Trap

Company TrapMe is offering a snap trap that reports online whether there is a catch or not. Local inspection of traps is not required any more[20].

Public space waste collection

In an effort to reduce waste in public space and cost of waste collection, city of Dún Laoghaire-Rathdown in Ireland decided to

---

[17] https://max.tkelevator.com/global-en/

[18] https://www.teliacompany.com/en/news/news-articles/2017/iot-sheep-in-norway/

[19] www.libelium.com

[20] https://trapme.io

replace all 530 traditional litter bins and installed 420 units of BigBelly IoT-enabled litter bins instead. Now, daily waste collection tours will be tailored according to transmitted fill level reports. This transformation decreased waste management efficiency by a total of 85% incl. reduction of dedicated collection staff and trucks[21].

Visitor Engagement Tracking

Wearables can be used to track user movement and behavior. Company Sirqui uses IoT techniques to understand visitor preferences, walking paths, duration of stay, queue lines of big events in stadiums or arenas. These insights can be used to take appropriate action for improvement of visitor experience[22].

IoT padlock

Company OpticalLock offers an IoT-enabled padlock which has a shackle that fits inside the eye rings designed for traditional locking mechanisms and provides IoT status alerts. It has sensors that detect motion, humidity, location, etc. When there's a change, the lock uses built-in cellular connectivity to send an alert[23].

Fire Protection for Forests

Dryad's LPWAN-based sensor network can detect wildfires and provide valuable insights into the microclimate and growth of the forest, i.e., actionable information for forest owners[24].

Smart Parking in Palo Alto, California

---

[21] www.bigbelly.com
[22] https://corp.sirqul.com
[23] www.opticallock.com
[24] www.dryad.net

City of Palo Alto (in Silicon Valley, near San Francisco) is using NB-IoT for a Smart City approach to avoid traffic congestions caused by cars go around and round the same block, in search of parking spots. Thus, sensors were installed at all the parking spots around the city. These sensors pass the occupancy status of each spot to the cloud. Any number of applications can consume that data. It can guide the drivers through the shortest route to an open spot[25].

Note: For further information and inspiration, more than 1000 different IoT use cases and cases studies are listed here: https://www.iotone.com/case-studies

2.3.2 Design Concepts for PSM and CE functions

Besides a professionally managed and maintained network, cellular LPWAN technologies will be first choice whenever high cell capacity, extra wide coverage range or deep inhouse resp. underground penetration will be required, esp. in use cases requiring battery driven IoT endpoint devices.

Both NB-IoT/LTE-M are providing a **power saving mode (PSM)** which are allowing a connected IoT device to switch off their RF transmitter and reduce power consumption to a few microamps during inactive periods. On top of that, NB-IoT/LTE-M allow to set additional **Coverage Extension (CE)** levels CE1 and CE2 for difficult-to-reach endpoint devices (either far away or barred by obstacles, walls, etc.). This mechanism works with error correction and repeated data transmission methods. But at the same time, use of CE levels reduces payload data rates significantly. Also, power

---

[25] https://www.paloaltonetworks.com/cyberpedia/smart-cities-in-the-age-of-5g-and-iot

consumption increases because required time for data transmission increases.[26] [27]

CE is not needed if an IoT device is located in an area with fair network signal strength. Some CIoT applications are requiring CE but might not require PSM because no strict power consumption limitations apply at the locations where the IoT device has been installed (e.g., for smart meter installations at basement floor with poor network coverage but a local power outlet) . As a consequence, any need for PSM and CE depends on IoT use case and the range of possible deployment locations for endpoint devices. If sometimes needed, sometimes not needed, the embedded IoT application must be prepared to manage PSM and CE network functions, i.e., it is **impacting the design of CIoT endpoint devices** (see Figure 3: Block diagram of a cellular IoT device). This differentiation leads to several application categories associated with CIoT devices which have been designed to use PSM functions or CE handling or both.

Typical CIoT applications are leveraging NB-IoT/LTE-M strengths and use **lowest-power and CE-enabled IoT devices** aiming at

- **monitoring** a remote environment or object (label: "Monitor"),
- **localization of** an object (label: "Localize"),
- submitting **alerts** in case an event occurs (label: "Alert") or
- providing an Internet **gateway** for a local IoT network (see extra section "Cellular Gateway").

For lowest-power CIoT devices, some uses cases are requiring a pre-installed non-rechargeable battery will power the IoT device, i.e., selected **battery capacity determines product lifetime**. This

---

[26] Olof Liberg, Marten Sundberg, Eric Wang, Johan Bergman, Joachim Sachs. Cellular Internet of Things. 2017. ISBN: 9780128124598

[27] https://iotcreators.com/docs/

requirement, for example, applies to installations in rural areas or wearables or object tracking applications. NB-IoT has been designed to guarantee 10+ years battery-driven operation, but only if the use case can reduce network activity to occasional or infrequent transmission of small data packages. Corresponding **activity periods** are either scheduled or triggered by an external event → IoT device will work in **push mode**, i.e., transmission of IoT payload data is initiated by the device. Or activity periods are requested via network → IoT device will work in **pull mode** i.e., transmission of IoT payload data is initiated by the user via Internet connection.

Figure 10 is showing how to categorize CIoT applications according to their need to support either PSM or CE or both. Application categories are labeled

- ("Application") = no PSM or CE handling required
- PSM "(Application") = PSM handling required
- PSM/CE ("Application") = both PSM and CE handling required

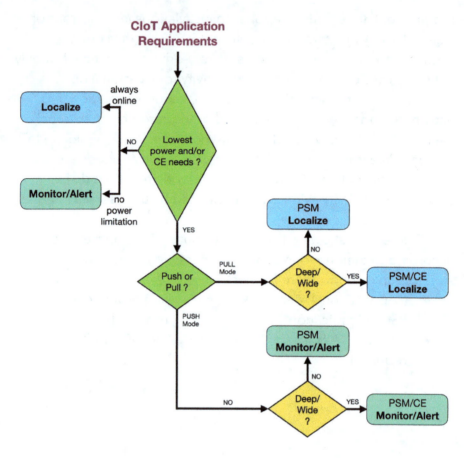

Figure 10: CIoT PSM/CE Application Categories

The following sections explain how to read the question tree which is presented in Figure 10 for different application scenarios "Locate", "Alert" and "Monitor".

Note: Detailed information how PSM and CE mechanisms work and how the cIoT device can negotiate related network parameters will be provided by *IoT Design Brief #2*, see [28]".

---

[28] Kersten Heins, Cellular IoT Devices - Network Interface, *IoT Design Briefs* book series (Book 2), 2023, ISBN: 9798374755350

2.3.2.1 "Monitor" and "Alert" Applications

Regardless of the target segment (refer to section "IoT Application Scope"), "Monitor" and "Alert" functions are fundamental IoT functions which are required for almost every IoT use case. Key objective is to inform IoT operators about remote environments or objects or warn them about critical events. Typical application examples are: **smart metering, surveillance, emission warning, asset utilization, service alert, home automation, fault detection, stock management, energy management, tamper detection, livestock monitoring, quality management, access control, smart buttons, recognition, inspection of infrastructure, leakage and flood detection, occupancy monitoring, outage detection, dead reckoning, trash management, smart parking, traffic control, predictive maintenance, patient monitoring, smart lighting, performance monitoring, crop yield improvement, tank monitoring, etc.**

Typical **"Monitor"** applications are keeping users aware of local conditions **periodically**, sending relevant information regularly once a day or every few hours, in a **"push" operating mode**. This is useful for remote equipment, an area or a site or any kind of object in an effort for information purposes or to identify problems requiring action. **Local parameters are measured** (e.g., moisture, temperature, position, acceleration, force, fill level, presence, motion, gas or liquid flow, light, power consumption, speed, altitude, light incidence, carbon monoxide, identity, heart rate), extracted, pre-processed in a way that meaningful and **actionable data is transmitted** to the IoT server.

From a functional point of view, **"Alert"** applications are similar to "Monitor" applications, but data transmission is triggered by an **event** rather than a fixed schedule (see Figure 11). This event typically is referring to a detected problem requiring immediate reaction by the IoT application, e.g., a parameter exceeding a certain threshold value or an unplanned presence of an object (incl. persons, animals, etc.) has been recognized

Any need for PSM and/or CE is determined by functional requirements and by the location where IoT devices will be installed. Typically, leveraging the specific strengths of cellular LPWAN network technology (esp. NB-IoT), typical CIoT application will be categorized as "PSM/CE Monitor/Alert" (see Figure 10).

After deployment of a stationary IoT device for "Monitor/Alert" applications, the installation procedure will first have to look for available network cells. If multiple network cells are within reach, the device will first have to evaluate applicable CE levels for each network and finally will have to decide which one to select. For devices with a fixed location, this process has to be executed only once and stay registered permanently on the selected network during its complete lifecycle. In order to minimize power consumption, the device will remain in PSM mode most of the time until an activity period is triggered by a fixed schedule or another event. In this case, the device will perform some additional sensing of local parameters and processing. Finally, the device will transmit requested IoT data and return to IDLE state. This procedure is illustrated in Figure 11:

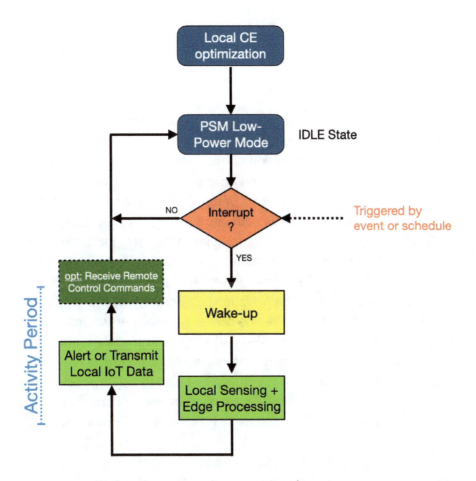

Figure 11: Activity loop for CIoT device in "push" mode

In addition to uplink transmission of IoT payload data and alerting the IoT application, IoT devices can also be used for **remote control** functions resp. local actions. For this purpose, the device can control actuators like a power switch, a valve, electric motor, etc. This task is **optional** and applies only to devices which have been built for remote control functions. For maximum efficiency, this task does not have to establish a power-consuming extra network connection. Instead, it uses an active RF period which is required for the main push data transmission anyway.

2.3.2.2 "Locate" Applications

For a "Locate" CIoT applications the main objective is to **determine the current position of an object**. A "Locate" CIoT application with an IoT position sensor device located in a well-covered area of the network and connected to a stationary power supply (or a regularly recharged battery) will not require any PSM or CE-related configuration. As a consequence, walking through our question tree in Figure 10 will end at label "Locate" indicating that PSM and CE features do not matter in this case.

For a "Locate" IoT application which has to continuously track and report the position of a travelling object in real-time, a built-in fixed battery cannot meet device power requirements. On top of frequent data transmission, NB-IoT is not recommended, if the tracked object is moving continuously across cell borders. For this use case, LTE-M offers a network cell-to-cell hand-over mechanisms similar which is also used by LTE for mobile phone communication, see "Table 2: Cellular Standards – IoT Application Requirements".

But for many "Locate" applications, the tracked object is movable but does not move all the time. Instead, it might change its location – occasionally and by purpose or by accident. For these type of use cases a **typical "Locate" use case** will ask for the actual position of an asset, good, material, inventory, containers, visitors either

1. **locally** e.g., within a production site to manage the material flow

or

2. **anywhere** or investigation of whereabouts of lost or stolen objects, e.g., valuable goods, shipment containers, expensive equipment.

For these two different application scenarios, localization approaches will be completely different. In case 1, determination of the current object position might be done by reading a barcode identifier (or a RFID tag) attacked to the tracked object on a routed path or from limited set of possible locations, i.e., a fixed path the object cannot leave. If used in industrial environments or for logistics, batteries for tracked objects will be recharged in a timely manner and will not cause any operational bottlenecks. When referring to Figure 10 this means that this use case is also categorized as a straight-forward "Locate" application which does not require any PSM or CE handling

In case 2, the actual position ("anywhere") will be completely unpredictable und must be determined from scratch, e.g., using an onboard GPS/GNSS satellite positioning assistance. By nature of this use case, an IoT module with a fixed pre-installed battery is required. If you cannot predict the actual location, CE might be needed, so we end up with application category "PSM/CE Locate", if not "PSM Locate" (see Figure 10).

Independent from CE need, for a "Locate" use case requiring a pre-installed battery, CIoT device will have to utilize the PSM feature in order to maximize device lifetime. "Locate" applications will have to work in **"pull" operating mode** because users will request the IoT device via network to inform about its actual location. This request will trigger a short pulling activity period which is illustrated in Figure 12.

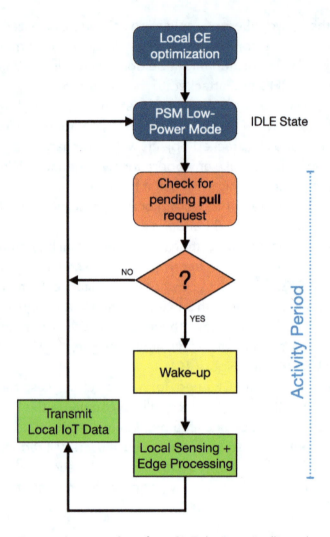

Figure 12: Activity loop for a CIoT device in "pull" mode

In order to minimize power consumption, the device will remain in PSM mode most of the time until an external wake up event via CIoT network will be detected. Pending requests to the device will be buffered by the cellular network and checked by the device regularly. Whenever a "locate" requests is recognized, the device will determine its position and perform some additional sensing of local parameters and processing. Finally, the device will transmit requested IoT data and return to IDLE state.

If the IoT device has not been moved, the "locate" request will be transmitted by the same cell as last time. But if it has been moved, the device will first have to look for available network cells. If multiple network cells are within reach, the device will first have to **evaluate applicable CE levels** for each network and finally will have to decide which one to select. For stationary devices, this process has to be executed only once (typically, after installation) and stay registered permanently. When referring to Figure 10 this means that this use case is categorized as "PSM/CE Localize" and used IoT devices will have to be designed accordingly.

2.3.3 Cellular Gateway

Another popular CIoT application is aiming at second-level IoT devices which are networked, but not connected directly to the Internet themselves. For example, some business-critical connected applications, e.g., for production process automation, customers are requiring an extra level of reliability and security, so they do not feel comfortable to handle in-house machine-to-machine (M2M) process communication between involved equipment through a shared public network. As a consequence, customers will prefer to set up a tailored inhouse local-area network (LAN) infrastructure for the critical part of the in-house M2M infrastructure.

On the other hand, wide-area (WAN) connectivity might be needed to interconnect distributed production facilities or to a central cloud service. This can be done by a cellular LPWAN access point combined with a gateway function which allows to interconnect LPWAN and inhouse proprietary network in a customer-defined manner. From an IoT perspective, this **IoT Gateway** might act as an IoT endpoint itself or pass messages to/from IoT devices connected via LAN or CAN bus or other interfaces used in industrial or consumer environments. Figure 13 illustrates the structure of an CIoT gateway.

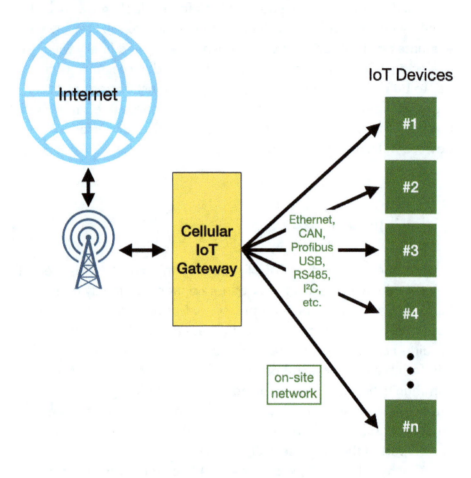

Figure 13: IoT Gateway Approach

Mission-critical applications in home or office environments with existing LAN connectivity are another target area for IoT gateways. For example, nation-wide rollout of smart power meters in Germany is specifying a central device called "Smart Meter Gateway (SMGW)" to be installed in more than 40 million German households and other electricity consumers[29]. For this application scenario, every commercial SMGW device will provide cellular connectivity as a fallback option in case other connectivity options are not available or an existing network installation fails to provide sufficient connectivity (e.g., for power meters located in underground basement). In fact, the SMGW is a quite complex IoT device providing cellular network connectivity and a couple of interfaces for internal connection of electricity meters as well as solar panels, car chargers, etc. SMGW devices have to comply with a specification which has been prepared by BSI institute on behalf of the German government. For each commercial SMGW product an evaluation and official approval is mandatory, which is covering quality of implemented mechanism for data security and tamper protection

---

[29] https://www.bsi.bund.de/EN/Themen/Unternehmen-und-Organisationen/Standards-und-Zertifizierung/Smart-metering/Smart-Meter-Gateway/smart-meter-gateway_node.html

3 Building Blocks of a CIoT Ecosystem

IoT use cases determine the technical requirements for IoT ecosystems, e.g., which local parameters are relevant for remote monitoring or which tasks are requiring "edge" processing power. In addition, case-by-case security requirements will determine which functions need to be implemented and at which level.

In fact, IoT ecosystems are different, and each of them has to be tailored for each application. But many common soft- and hardware ingredients are available as **configurable standard products** in a way that they can be used for many IoT applications.

3.1 IoT Design with off-the-shelf elements

Good news for IoT project owners is that the design of a (secure) IoT device has never been easier because many essential hardware building blocks and other ingredients (driver software, communication protocol stacks, IoT clouds, etc.) are offered as **versatile components and services**. Instead of developing a custom product which are dedicated to address the customer application, standard products are offering a comprehensive set of features which are outnumbering the individual customer requirements for a specific design project. Instead of designing a tailored ecosystem from scratch, the IoT application designer will "just" have to develop an appropriate software configuration in order to activate required functions and deactivate functions which are not needed. Even if a standard product might not be the perfectly tailored solution for every IoT project, it will reduce development effort, speed up time-to-market and reduce overall cost. From a customer perspective, the **standard-product-based design approach** particularly pays off for low-to-medium-scale projects with a demand of less than 100k units p.a.

Standard hardware products are so-called ASSPs. What is an ASSP? An **ASSP** stands for **A**pplication-**S**pecific **S**tandard **P**roduct. It is an active chip component which has been designed to address a specific electronic application (e.g., a cellular network interface). In contrary to customer-specific ASICs (ASIC=Application-Specific Integrated Circuit) which is owned by the user of this chip, an ASSP is designed to be used by different customers and offered for sale by chip manufacturers. The ASSP business model is based on the business assumption that the addressed target application will be an appealing market for **many customers** – leading to high volumes and sales numbers.

For the chip manufacturer, a fundamental success enabler is a powerful external sales channel allowing them to focus on design, documentation, online support, product marketing, but to delegate direct customer interaction. Typical ASSPs for use in (secure) cellular IoT device designs are illustrated in Figure 14. For cellular IoT projects, ASSPs and services are available for these categories:

- Host Microcontrollers and Security Elements
- Cellular Network Interface Modules and SIMs
- Sensors (and actuators)
- IoT clouds

The following sections are providing an overview of ASSP and cloud candidates for cellular IoT ecosystem concepts.

<u>Note:</u> Further technical details, a market overview and selection criteria for network interface modules are provided in *IoT Design Brief #2* , see [30].

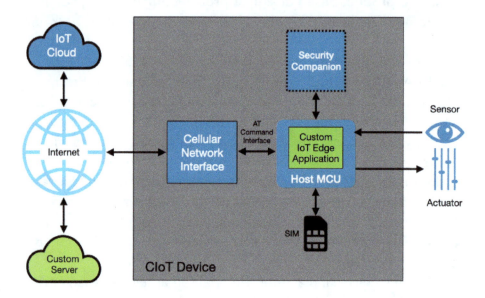

Figure 14: ASSPs and cloud service for cellular IoT devices

3.1.1 Host MCU

The host MCU has a central role because here the **embedded part of the IoT application** is located which determines the functionality of the IoT device and masters all external local interactions. In particular, the host MCU controls the operation of the network interface aka modem ASSP (network sockets, protocols, etc.) via AT command interface. In addition, IoT peripherals (esp. sensors and actuators) are controlled, scheduled and payload data

---

[30] Kersten Heins, Cellular IoT Devices - Network Interface, *IoT Design Briefs* book series (Book 2), 2023, ISBN: 9798374755350

will be retrieved and pre-processed according to IoT application requirements.

Typically, a simple low-cost general-purpose MCU will meet basic functional requirements have sufficient processing power to run the embedded IoT software as long as standard interfaces like UART serial port or USB (for the modem ASSP), an I²C/SPI bus (for sensors) and a couple of GPIOs are offered. USB is also used for connection with development environment or test tools.

On top of that, for battery-driven operation, a suitable MCU should have efficient power-management functions, **low-power** modes, and a **wake-up function** to be triggered from external sources (pin). For monitoring functions (e.g., battery charge level, intrusion detection), the MCU should offer an **analog-to-digital-converter** (ADC) and a **watchdog timer**. For mission-critical alert IoT devices (see section <u>"Monitor" and "Alert" Applications</u>"), a **short interrupt latency** might be required.

The IoT application program is containing sensitive processing information and intellectual property which is requiring protection against eavesdropping. An embedded **read/write protectable memory** which is large enough to store the IoT application program as well as IoT payload data and an event log file. A one-time-programmable (OTP) part of the internal memory is useful for keeping an immutable device identifier or product lifecycle status.

These are just a few functions to meet basic security requirements of a typical IoT ecosystem. For advanced protection of assets and strong crypto-backed device authentication and confidentiality of transmitted data, dedicated hardware support might be required. An external security coprocessor is an option, but also **secure MCUs** are available (see section "<u>Security</u>") to replace a standard MCU.

3.1.2 Sensors

Sensing one or multiple parameters of a remote location is a major ingredient of every IoT application. Typical parameters to be monitored are temperature, humidity, pressure, vibration, motion, fill level, weight, noise, volume, applied force, chemical composition, presence, distance, brightness, speed. But also, a simple yes/no digital signal can be used, e.g., an electromechanical switch or an interrupted current flow through a conducting lead indicating an open door, presence of an object, a certain fill level, etc.

Usually, sensors are offering either analog or digital interfaces and typically connected to the host MCU (see Figure 14). Three different interface options are common: general-purpose digital I/Os (GPIOs), an integrated Analog/Digital Converter (ADC) and I²C or SPI serial data interfaces. A simple digital yes/no indicator can connect to a GPIO pin of the module. For analog signals, an ADC channel can be used. Digital sensors normally use an I²C or SPI interface for data transmission.

As a starting point for a new IoT project, some selection tools are offering an excellent vehicle for competitive comparison, available online from large distributors like Arrow[31], Avnet[32]. Digi-Key[33] or Mouser[34] (in alphabetical order). After choosing of the sensor category (temperature, humidity, motion, gas flow, etc.), filters can be used to narrow selection by parameters like resolution, interface, operating temperature, accuracy, packaging, etc.

Application Examples:

---

[31] https://www.arrow.com/en/products/search?cat=Sensors

[32] https://www.avnet.com/shop/emea/c/sensors-transducers

[33] https://www.digikey.com/en/products/category/sensors-transducers/25

[34] https://eu.mouser.com/c/sensors/

Many sensors are directly matching the objective of an IoT application. For example, for remote monitoring of CO_2 pollution, specialized sensor ICs are available to deliver the actual **CO_2 rate** in a digital format. Integration of these sensors via I^2C bus is straight-forward.

Other applications can use sensor outputs as an input parameter for calculations, e.g., to determine the distance to an object. For this purpose, the **time-of-flight (TOF)** of an emitted light pulse and reflected by the object. A sensor detects the returning signal, and the total travel time determines its distance to the object.

Another example are MEMS sensors (MEMS = micro-electro-mechanical systems) which are based on semiconductor technology to measure mechanical force, i.e. convert it into an electrical signal. In fact, **MEMS accelerometers** measure linear acceleration. But they can also be used for specific purposes such as inclination and vibration measurements which are needed for "Predictive Maintenance" of machines or equipment. With MEMS accelerometers you can also address special IoT use cases, e.g., detect an object which has been moved from its assigned location, or detect free-falling condition of an object. Sensor measurement data might not immediately answer the question, but measurement data can be used to feed calculation and creation of meaningful IoT data.

3.1.3 Cellular Network Interface Modules

Interfacing to a cellular network is complex and requires advanced RF and analog design expertise. On top of this, application developers expect a certain level of abstraction from complex 3GPP standards resp. from low-level knowledge of network physical layer, device-network synchronization, random-access procedures, etc. Know-how on this level is useful but not required for IoT application development. Instead, for efficient work, higher-level functions (API) and efficient tools are needed. Cellular modem vendors have recognized an increasing IoT demand from different industry segments, so they started to leverage their modem expertise for their offer of **comprehensive and easy-to-use subsystems**, incl. libraries for (secure) network protocols, cloud support, etc. A cellular network module is a key building block of every CIoT ecosystem (recall Figure 14), they have been designed for IoT application developers requiring cellular connectivity for their project without spending too much time with underlying cellular network technology itself.

In fact, core of each cellular network module is a **modem** (modulator-demodulator), i.e., a data converter which is modulating a carrier wave to encode digital data for transmission (recall Figure 4). In our case, transmission medium is a wireless cellular network with carrier frequencies of up to 2GHz and output transmit power of up to 23dBm resp. 200 mW (for NB-IoT). This mix of digital, analog, and power requirements means extra challenge for integration within a single semiconductor product. In the end, cellular network interface modules are usually containing a mixed-signal modem chip plus extra power amplifier and some other discrete components altogether in a compact **multi-chip SMD package** (e.g., a 96- pin LGA with 16x26x2.4 mm). This method of bundling multiple integrated circuits (ICs) and passive components into a single package is called System-in-Package (SiP). A typical cellular network module contains (see block diagram Figure 15):

- Modem incl. command/data interface to IoT application (UART or USB)
- RF interface, amplifiers, filters
- Clock generation and distribution
- Power Management
- SIM card interface
- Microcontroller, OS, firmware, memory
- Analog/Digital Converter
- Peripheral interfaces (GPIOs, I^2C, SPI, etc.)

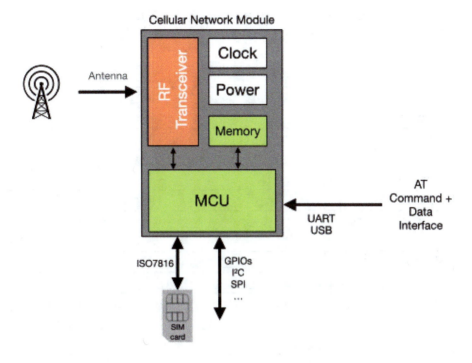

Figure 15: Cellular Network Interface Module – Block Diagram

In fact, these network interface modules are very popular electronic components and the functional heart of most cellular IoT devices. According to market researcher IoT Analytics, the global cellular IoT module market grew by 15x between 2010 and 2022, with approximately **2.5 billion modules shipped by the end of 2022**[35]. According to market researcher Counterpoint, **quarterly shipment of 100 million** IoT modules has been exceeded in Q2/2021 for the first time [36].

---

[35] https://iot-analytics.com/iot-modules

[36] https://www.counterpointresearch.com/global-cellular-iot-module-shipments-q2-2021/

This is a list of cellular IoT module manufacturers (non-exhaustive, in alphabetical order):

Company	URL
Cavli Wireless	www.cavliwireless.com/iot-modules/
Fibocom	www.fibocom.com/en/products/list_lcid_124.html
MeiG	en.meigsmart.com/product/wifimz67.html
Nordic Semiconductor	www.nordicsemi.com/Products/Low-power-cellular-IoT
Quectel	www.quectel.com/lpwa-iot-modules
Sierra Wireless	www.sierrawireless.com/iot-modules/lpwa-modules/
SIMcom	www.simcom.com/module
Telit	www.telit.com/cellular-lpwa/
Thales	www.thalesgroup.com/en/markets/digital-identity-and-security/iot/iot-connectivity/products/iot-products
u-blox	www.u-blox.com/en/cellular-modules

Note: Telit recently acquired Thales' IoT portfolio. Both product lines will be merged under the umbrella of a new company called Telit Cinterion[37] soon.

Typically, CIoT modules are bundled with comprehensive software packages including firmware components for network connection and (secure) data transmission (e.g., sockets, protocols). Manufacturers are supporting customer CIoT deployments by cloud services for IoT data processing as well as device management incl. a public-key infrastructure (PKI) and provisioning. On top of that, some modules are supporting development of a customer application to be uploaded and executed by the module MCU subsystem.

---

[37] https://www.telit.com/press/telit-and-thales-announce-the-creation-of-the-leading-western-iot-solutions-provider-telit-cinterion/

3.1.3.1 SIM – eSIM – iSIM

By nature, every CIoT device needs Internet connectivity - which is provided by an external service provider. In fact, every cellular device is identified on the mobile network by identification data stored in its SIM card (SIM = Subscriber Identification Module). This fundamental fact applies also to cellular IoT devices. In fact, each SIM is internationally identified by its integrated circuit card identifier (ICCID). The ICCID is the identifier of the actual SIM card itself whereas the mobile subscriber identity (IMSI) number – in combination with a unique authentication key – is used for identification of the user device on mobile networks.

A SIM card is a personalized electronic component which is associated to the selected connectivity partner, i.e., a network operator (MNO) or network service provider (MVNO). The SIM is used to identify the user, and it activates a pre-configured, operator-specific connection profile on the user device. Each **profile** is "owned" by an operator and contains all relevant operator data related to a subscription, including the operator's credentials, and booked SIM based applications or services. Based on a commercial agreement (subscription plan) with the user, the selected network partner defines which network services will be available and will deliver booked services using a combination of their own and/or sub-contracted mobile networks.

For a cellular IoT device, a SIM card is usually inserted during production or installation and will stay there until its end of life. But for some IoT projects, flexibility of MNO selection during the device lifecycle definitely would make sense. A fixed profile selection, for example, would be a problem if devices are used in markets where permanent roaming is prohibited by regulation, such as in China and Brazil. Another reason is operational cost: even if an MNO offers roaming in an area which is not covered by its own network, flexible selection of another local network might offer IoT connectivity at a lower price.

Swapping SIM cards is a logistical challenge esp. for large-scale IoT projects where you might have different MNO preferences for installed IoT devices at different locations. From a technical point of view, a SIM card is just a copy-protected secure 32-64kByte storage device which is owned and managed exclusively by the MNO. But in order to increase flexibility and reduce cost, industry members have been pushing to "virtualize" the SIM card. Result is an **embedded SIM (eSIM)** or **eUICC** (embedded universal integrated circuit card) which converts the removable SIM card into a downloadable software profile to run on a suitable secure chip platform, e.g., a discrete SMD-packaged eUICC which is attached (i.e., non-removably) into the user device during production. In fact, the eUICC allows loading of multiple **digital profiles**, so that users can select and activate the most appropriate profile remotely. The eSIM standardization is being facilitated by GSM Association [38]. An eSIM can accommodate **several subscriptions**, and provisioning of an eSIM can be performed over-the-air with clearly defined roles and interfaces described in GSMA's "Remote SIM Provisioning (RSP) Technical Specification" [39]. High security standards for production and processes have been put in place in order to create confidence among all involved parties, i.e., chip manufacturers, device manufacturers, operators, service providers and users.

The eSIM approach is addressing the patchwork and fragmented structure of the current global cellular network and it allow **new distributions models for digital operator profiles**, e.g., via scanning a QR code during installation of a CIoT device. For current IoT applications an eSIM will efficiently solve logistics problems in case a different MNO should be used. But eSIM might also create new ideas for new IoT business opportunities because it will allow IoT application owners to switch to the most appropriate network anywhere at any time – on the fly.

---

[38] https://www.gsma.com/esim/esim-specification/
[39] https://www.gsma.com/esim/wp-content/uploads/2021/07/SGP.22-v2.3.pdf

From a practical CIoT device design point of view, use of an eSIM will **reduce component count** and PCB space, and obsolete SIM connectors will increase security and reliability of the design. Impact on power consumption will be marginal because SIM card will be powered by the modem only when needed. Next evolution step is an **integrated SIM (iSIM)** which is allowing to incorporate UICC functionality on chip level into an existing tamper-proof system-on-chip (SOC) design, e.g., a CC certified secure element or a secure microcontroller (see section "Security").

Massive eSIM/iSIM adoption is ongoing and used by many mobile phones but, it is also offered by an increasing number of IoT cellular network modules.

Note: Further technical details about CIoT modules and SIM components and an up-to-date product comparison is included in *IoT Design Brief #2* , see [40]".

3.1.4 IoT Security

Very often, the need to implement any security measures is not obvious and gently pushed aside by manufacturers of CIoT endpoint devices. It is true that security is not available for free, but it this investment is less expensive compared to damages caused by a lack of security. In general, **IoT attacks are skyrocketing**[41], but they are driven by various intentions. Fraud is one example, industrial spying is another. And privacy protection (of IoT users) is prescribed by national laws and therefor mandatory anyway. In fact, a decent **risk assessment** will have to identify scenarios for potential attacks for each IoT use case. Results will determine which **countermeasures** to implement – and at which level of strength. In most cases, use of cryptographic methods and an infrastructure for generation and a

---

[40] Kersten Heins, Cellular IoT Devices - Network Interface, *IoT Design Briefs* book series (Book 2), 2023, ISBN: 9798374755350

[41] https://threatpost.com/iot-attacks-doubling/169224/

decent management of IoT credentials (i.e., a public-key-infrastructure - PKI) will be needed.

A CIoT ecosystem comprises several elements which are potentially vulnerable: network, cloud, devices (recall Figure 2: IoT Ecosystem"). All of them should contribute to the overall protection of the IoT application. The good news for IoT project owners is that, for a cellular IoT network, a certain level of security will be managed and guaranteed by professional network service providers. Same applies to the central IoT application if the involved server platform is managed by an external professional service provider. Typically, this service is running in a cloud environment (see section "IoT Clouds"). As a consequence, IoT project owners will "just" have to select network and cloud partners carefully, then **focus on secure CIoT device design** in order to meet required security objectives for the overall IoT ecosystem.

Very often, IoT devices will have to work in public or unattended areas which are not controlled by the IoT service provider. In these cases, IoT devices are exposed to potential attackers and more vulnerable than an IoT server located in a safe environment. This is an extra challenge and must be considered carefully during specification of a secure IoT device. In general, a secure IoT frontend device design will have to ensure

- Safeguarding stored credentials and intellectual property incl. protection against physical intrusion
- Secure execution of the embedded IoT application
- Reliable operation of connected peripherals (sensors, actuators)
- Establishment of a secure end-to-end communication channel to the IoT application server

In fact, the IoT device executes sensitive embedded software and processes sensitive IoT data which is finally transmitted to a safe place for further analysis. All credentials and cryptographic key material used for secure communication with the server are stored inside the IoT device.

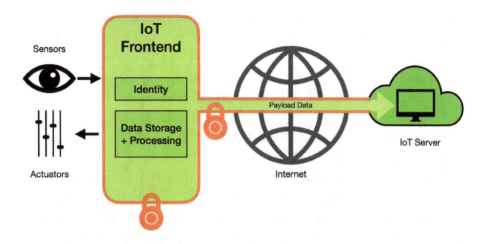

Figure 16: IoT Frontend Security

Figure 16 illustrates the objective of security measures to be applied to the IoT device including communication channel to the server. Depending on the use case, the device might also need protection against physical intrusion or software attacks or attempts to exploit data leaks via side-channel attacks or fault injections. In the end, the device will act as a secure frontend device which is covering the complete installation of a local IoT application.

In order to ensure bullet-proof communication of sensitive data and remote control of IoT devices, IoT projects will have to implement an appropriate level of security and protection against potential attacks or attempts to misuse the IoT application. Independent from technology used for data transmission, a secure channel between communication partners will have to protect integrity and confidentiality of data. This **end-to-end security** will ensure that nobody can understand or modify data transferred from one endpoint to another (typically from an IoT device to a dedicated IoT server or vice versa). For this purpose, data encryption is used - to an IoT server which is located in a safe environment. In addition, both parties will have to mutually authenticate each other before starting any communication session. The IoT device will have to handle secure storage and processing of involved cryptographic keys. On top of this, IoT devices which are used in risky environments will require extra protection against physical intrusion.

For use in CIoT endpoint devices, all vendors of cellular network modules are including features or options to support **TLS (Transport Layer Security)**, the successor of SSL (Secure Sockets Layer). TLS is a secure communication protocol which is using public-key cryptography. For a straight-forward implementation of an end-to-end-security approach, the TLS/SSL software stack bundled with the IoT network module can be used. In this case, key storage and crypto operations will be performed by the module MCU.

Depending on identified threats, potential damage and expected attacker profiles (skills, equipment), an advanced level of protection might be required. For this purpose, dedicated hardware can provide extra crypto performance and quality, e.g., a true random number generator. On top of that, proven tamper-resistance offers secure storage for key material and a secure processing environment for critical crypto operations. Standardized **security evaluation schemes** (e.g., Common Criteria, SESIP and PSA Certified) by independent labs are used to verify efficiency and strengths of implemented protection mechanisms. Certified security is offered by **secure microcontrollers** as well as by so-called **secure elements** which are originated from smartcard technology. For critical IoT applications, these components can be used for extra reliable system operation and bullet-proof IoT trustability [42].

---

[42] Kersten Heins. Trusted Cellular IoT Devices. Dec. 2022. Springer International Publishing

3.1.5 Online Support + Supply Channel

Good news for IoT application developers is that the "Internet of Things" has been selected by all market players as the #1 top priority application for the IT electronics business. All contributors like semiconductor manufacturers, network operators, distributors, IT service providers, etc. are trying to benefit from promising IoT market outlook and to take their share. For IoT device designers this means that they can expect to receive a decent level of support for their engineering work.

On top of this, most **manufacturers of (IoT) electronic components** and subsystems have learned how to handle a large number of different customer projects via sales partners or online channels. In fact, most chips are offered as standard products accompanied by a **comprehensive set of documentation**, evaluation tools and a design kit. Objective is to provide self-explanatory material which is supposed to answer most questions in order to minimize customer need for one-to-one support. All relevant product information is **published online and downloadable** via manufacturer website. Usually, manufacturers also allow customers to **order** product samples, evaluation boards, design kits, etc. **directly through their website**. Some are also providing volume prices and direct online ordering.

In addition, and whenever needed, an **authorized dealer (distributor)** will be the day-to-day business partner and entry-point for all kind of customer requests. Table 3 provides a non-exhaustive list of distributors for IoT components. Distributors typically work with different product lines from different manufacturers. Besides their major objective to handle volume orders with minimum lead times, traditional distributors are acting independently and work as a supply partner offering additional customer services incl. stock management, application expertise and technical support (marked with an "S" in Table 3). For those who are asking for **regional support**, some distributors are offering websites for target countries, e.g., **Sanshin** for Japanese customers or **Changnam** in Korean language.

In the meantime, most distributors have prepared themselves for IoT-specific customer requests. For example, **Arrow** and **Future Electronics** are offering dedicated IoT solutions and services. On top of their role as a dealer, some are dedicated IoT distributors positioning themselves as IoT consultants and **IoT system integrators**, e.g., **Telic** or **Elproma** (marked with a "B" in Table 3).

As an alternative to skilled IoT distributors, commercial customer requests can also go to **online distributors** who do not offer any additional support, but very competitive prices (marked with an "O" in Table 3). **Digi-Key** is one of them but offers an online discussion board aka online forum (marked by an "F" in Table 3). **Avnet** is offering even two discussion boards. Others like **SOS Electronics** and **Symmetry** are informing their customers with their own blog (marked with a "B" in Table 3).

Distributor Name	O= Online only S= Support I= Integrator F= Discussion Board (Forum) B= Blog	Homepage
Arrow	S	www.arrow.com/en/iot
Avnet (incl. Abacus, EBV, Element14, Farnell, Newark, Silica)	S, 2x F	www.avnet.com, community.element14.com, www.hackster.io
Changnam	S	http://www.changnam.com
Digi-Key	O, F	www.digikey.com, forum.digikey.com

(continued)

Elproma	S, I	www.elpromaelectronics.com/en/
Future Electronics	S	www.futureelectronics.com/en/our-solutions/iot-solutions
Glyn	S	www.glyn.com.au
Mouser	O	www.mouser.com
RS Components	S	www.rs-components.com
Rutronik	S	www.rutronik.com
Sanshin	S	www.sanshin.co.jp/en/solution/iot/
SOS Electronics	S, B	www.soselectronic.com, www.soselectronic.com/articles
Symmetry	S, B	www.symmetryelectronics.com, www.symmetryelectronics.com/blog/
Telic	S, I	www.telic.de/en
Wintech	S	www.wincomponents.com

Table 3: Distributors for IoT components

IoT design engineers are particularly online-minded and might take decisions to use certain components based on information they have extracted from online sources. For system designers, **manufacturer websites** are most important **self-service repositories** for product information and a common starting point to prepare for competitive product comparisons. Besides technical information like datasheets and user manuals also white papers, presentations and videos are available for download from manufacturer websites. Dedicated design kits should include drivers, sample source code, schematics, guidelines for PCB layout, etc. For components like cellular network modules or sensors which are specifically addressing IoT devices, many manufacturers are offering **IoT-specific application notes and design tips** in order to support implementation and to speed up customer time-to-market. In particular, they should explain how to perform application-specific adjustments, e.g., which features have been implemented to save power consumption and/or how to configure a NB-IoT network cell according to requirements of an IoT application (e.g., for maximum performance or low latency).

On top of product information, manufacturers should offer **interactive support services**. A popular online support instrument is a virtual community where people with a particular common interest meet online and exchange information. For this purpose, manufacturers of electronic components offer a community platform with discussion boards for product-related topics. These are places where users can ask questions and share material with other community members. **Communities** are managed by a company moderator and supported by product experts, but key aspect for success are contributions from other users. Community members will have to register, but hide their professional identity from others, i.e., they can participate anonymously. By nature, all contributions are published and might help multiple visitors. For non-public support requests, some manufacturers are offering the option to submit a **private support ticket**. Each case will be handled one-to-one by a company employee and will be escalated to a product expert, if required.

3.1.6 IoT Clouds

By nature, IoT applications are connected to the Internet, exchanging data between IoT clients (devices) and an **IoT server**. During field operation, the IoT server will collect data from deployed IoT devices and perform further data processing according to application requirements. **IoT data consolidation and analysis** will generate actionable insights or remote-control commands to the IoT device, if applicable. In any case, the IoT server will have to be managed by the respective IoT business owner, but on-site operation might be difficult to cope for large-scale IoT deployments with many devices and big data load. As an alternative for this purpose, professionally managed and dedicated IoT clouds are offered by external parties.

Another challenge is to **manage deployed devices** in the field, i.e., to check status, update functionality or to re-configure them, if required. But also, during IoT device production, external services will be required to perform **device provisioning** and injection of an individual device identity (Root-of-Trust).

An IoT project can take advantage of external online IoT services instead of implementing them in-house, e.g., server hosting, a **public-key-infrastructure (PKI)**, IoT device management, data analytics. An IoT cloud offers resources (servers, storage) and configurable functions for IoT applications and services to support deployment of IoT devices. In general, IoT cloud services are leveraging available external expertise of IT companies and offload inhouse development efforts to build an infrastructure for IoT device provisioning, management, and data processing. IoT cloud services allow IoT applications to select from a collection of options to collect, filter, transform, visualize, and act upon device data according to customer-defined rules.

Following increasing worldwide demand for IoT solutions, big IT players like Google or AWS have entered this market. In addition, some hardware manufacturers of cellular network modules are bundling cloud services with their products in an effort to offer a one-stop-shopping experience to their customers, including

- **generic IoT cloud functions** like data analysis, reporting
- **PKI services** for secure IoT data transmission incl. device authentication and identity management
- Remote **device management** incl. provisioning and firmware updates
- **security-as-a-service (SaaS)** online functions offloading some complex crypto work from the IoT device.

But in order to offer maximum flexibility to their customers, most of them are also supporting mentioned 3rd-party IoT clouds. In order to support a large variety of IoT applications, **3rd-party IoT clouds** are versatile and generic, i.e., offered services are working independently from target application and device hardware or used network technology. Cloud services do interact on low-level directly with device hardware or operating system. Instead, on device side a secure network socket (typically TLS) is acting as a device identifier and endpoint for IoT cloud one-to-one communication.

For most IoT clouds, HTTP or MQTT application layer protocols can be used for uplink IoT data transfer or for downlink device updates. Embedded HTTP and/or MQTT clients are standard firmware functions offered by most cellular network modules. This means that the device MCU will communicate with the device network socket via its AT command interface and manage all data transmission of the IoT device with the IoT cloud. Figure 17 is illustrating the interface and major IoT cloud functions.

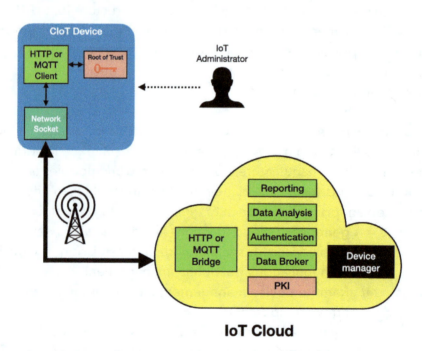

Figure 17: CIoT Cloud Interface and Functions

During initialization in production or during field operation, a device management function can be used to set up or change individual device configurations incl. its Root-of-Trust incl. a unique identifier, firmware updates, etc. It also maintains a logical configuration of each device and can be used to remotely control the device from the cloud. Since the IoT cloud does not know any technical details of the IoT device, each configuration request is must be converted locally by the host MCU into a sequence of module-specific AT commands. Available functions will be mainly determined by the customer IoT device, e.g., by embedded software stacks and initial device provisioning.

This a non-exhaustive list of third-party IoT clouds (in alphabetical order):

- AWS IoT Core, URL: https://aws.amazon.com/iot-core/
- Google Cloud IoT Core, URL: https://cloud.google.com/iot-core
- Microsoft Azure IoT, URL: https://azure.microsoft.com/en-us/overview/iot/
- Telekom Cloud of Things, URL: https://iot.telekom.com/en/solutions/platform

Cellular IoT - Glossary

Description of frequently used technical terms and acronyms related to the Internet of Things and cellular network technology.

Note: **bold** items indicate terms with its own description in this glossary.

Term	Acronym	Description
3rd Generation Partnership Project	3GPP	Global standardization body for cellular mobile telecommunication protocols like **LTE**
Access Point Name	APN	Name of a gateway between a **3GPP** cellular network and the Internet. Typically, also contains the an operator identifier (**MNO** or **MVNO**)
Actuator		IoT device component, which is performing a physical action, e.g., a motor, a switch, a valve or a pump
Advanced Encryption Standard	AES	Algorithm used for symmetric cryptography
Application-Specific Standard Products	ASSP	Standard chip component addressing a specific electronic application (e.g., a cellular network interface). In contrary to customer-specific ASICs, an ASSP is designed to be used by different customers.

Asymmetric cryptography		See Public-key cryptography
AT Command Interface		Standard network programming interface (**API**) used for interaction with a **modem**
Application Programming Interface	API	Specific software connection offering services to other software modules
Authentication		Process of verifying the identity of a person of networked object
Bill of Material	BOM	List of the parts, and the quantities of each needed to manufacture an end product.
Coverage Enhancement	CE	Methods to improve **LTE-M** and **NB-IoT** cellular network reach using repeated data transmissions and **HARQ** error correction
Bluetooth		Short-range radio access communication standard
Cellular IoT	CIoT	IoT based on cellular network technology
Central Processing Unit	CPU	Executes instructions of a computer program. Core of a **microcontroller (MCU)**
Certificate		Short for public-key certificate
Certification Authority	CA	Trusted 3rd-party entity that issues **digital certificates** for a user group
Chain of Trust		A layered structure of certificates/signatures (based on a trust anchor) assuring the trustworthiness of other

		elements within the structure. Validity of each layer is guaranteed by the previous layer to create a chain.
Checksum		A small, easy to calculate digital value representing the larger original file, e.g., to be used to verify its **integrity**
Constrained Application Protocol	CoAP	**TCP/IP** Application-layer network protocol
Common Criteria	CC	Standard for security evaluations
Common Criteria Evaluation Assurance Level	CC EAL	Certified security confidence level following a completed product evaluation according to **Common Criteria** rules
Countermeasures		Process or implementations that can prevent or mitigate the actions of a threat or an attack
Cyberattack		Offensive maneuver against computer systems, networks, infrastructures
Cyber-physical system		Networked embedded system, which is tightly coupled with physical processes, i.e., the foundation of an **IoT ecosystem**
Decryption		Process of using a cryptographic algorithm to convert encrypted data (**ciphertext**) back into original data (**plaintext**)
Data Encryption Standard	DES	Algorithm used for **symmetric cryptography**. Not used any more.

Denial-of-service attack	DoS	**Cyberattack** to make a network resource unavailable, e.g., by overloading it with superfluous requests
Diffie-Hellmann	DH	Handshake protocol and algorithm to create a shared secret key (session key) for a secure communication channel - based by exchanging public information between both parties.
Digital Certificate		See Public-key certificate
Digital Signature		Mathematical scheme for verifying the **authenticity** and the **integrity** of digital messages or documents.
Digital Twin		Virtual representation of a physical asset, e.g., an IoT device. The twin is continuously updated to mirror the current state of the physical thing.
Edge Computing		Distributed computing paradigm that brings computation and data storage closer to the sources of data. IoT follows this idea.
Extended Discontinuous Reception	eDRX	Extended DRX power saving feature for **LTE** networks which is turning off the RF when not used
Elliptic Curve Cryptography	ECC	Algorithm used for **public-key cryptography** based on elliptical curve constraints.
Encryption		Process of using a cryptographic algorithm to

		convert original data (**plaintext**) into incomprehensible data (**ciphertext**).
End-to-end encryption	E2EE	Communication system where only the communicating users can read the messages – using cryptographic keys needed to decrypt the conversation which are accessible by communication users only.
evolved NodeB	eNodeB (eNB)	In LTE networks similar to a GSM base station
Entropy		Quality of a random number (unpredictability)
Embedded SIM	eSIM	Software-based integrated SIM card, e.g., into a cellular network interface chip
Fault Injection Attack	FI	Attack method to change behavior of a system by exposing it with extreme conditions, e.g., clock glitches or higher temperature or supply voltage
Federal Information Processing Standards	FIPS	Standards set by the US government for data protection.
Firmware		Embedded software stored in non-volatile memory of a computing device
Firmware over-the-air	FOTA	Technical approach for remote updating the **firmware** of an (IoT) device via wireless network
Fog Computing		Same as **Edge Computing**

Gateway		A Internet device used in IoT ecosystems to manage internal data transfer via different interfaces and protocols
General Data Protection Regulation	GDPR	EU law on data protection and privacy in European Union
General Packet Radio Service	GPRS	2G/3G cellular mobile data service with low data rates and continuous connection to the Internet
GitHub		GitHub.com is a hosting platform for software development, commonly used for open-source software projects where users can download latest versions and documentation.
Geofencing		IoT use case – typically GPS-based – that works with virtual boundaries around a physical area in order to trigger an action of an IoT device
Global Positioning System, Global Navigation Satellite System	GPS, GNSS	Satellite-based radio navigation systems
Hybrid automatic repeat request	HARQ	LTE process combining data retransmission and error correction
Hash function		Mathematical function used to map data of arbitrary size to fixed-size values, e.g., a message digest.
International Mobile Equipment Identity	IMEI	Unique code consisting of 14 digits and a check digit for

		identifying **3GPP**-based mobile devices. The IMEI code is attached to the **MT**.
Industrial IoT	IIoT	IoT solutions aiming at industrial resp. B-to-B applications
Industrial, Scientific, and Medical Band	ISM	An unlicensed part of the RF spectrum used for general purpose data communications. 2.4 GHz is the global unlicensed frequency
Integrated Circuit	IC	Active electronic component integrating multiple functional elements into one single semiconductor-based device
Integrity		Assurance that (transmitted) data has not been altered, modified, or replaced.
Internet Protocol Suite	TCP/IP	Set of communication protocols how to format, address, transmit data. Four abstraction layers: Link, Internet, Transport and Application layers.
International mobile subscriber identity	IMSI	Unique identifier for mobile user, assigned by MNO in SIM resp. eSIM
IoT Cloud		On-demand IT services to facilitate IoT devices incl. collection, analysis, processing of IoT data
IoT Ecosystem		Ingredients of an IoT system consisting of sensors/actuators, an edge application, network connectivity, server-based

		application software and security measures. Based on a **cyber-physical system**
Key		A parameter, such as a private key, public key, secret key or session key that is used in cryptographic functions
Key Pair		Corresponding public and private keys, used for **Public-key cryptography**
Key Management		Management of cryptographic keys in a cryptosystem including the generation, exchange, storage, use, crypto-shredding (destruction) and replacement of keys
Key Schedule		An algorithm that creates subkeys in cipher blocks within a given **key space**
Logical attack		Type of **cyberattack** which is performed remotely, i.e., by software via an vulnerable **API**
(Long Range)	LoRa	Proprietary, non-cellular **LPWAN** technology, in unlicensed spectrum
Low-power wide area network	LPWAN	Category of long-range wireless networks technologies, e.g., **NB-IoT** and **LTE-M**
Long-Term Evolution	LTE	Standard for wireless broadband communication, developed by **3GPP**
Long-Term Evolution - Machine	LTE-M	Cellular LPWAN technology based on **3GPP** LTE standard
Machine-to-Machine	M2M	Direct communication between network devices

Man-in-the-middle attack		**Cyberattack** where the attacker sits between two communication partners and eavesdrops or alters transmitted data
Maximum Coupling Loss	MCL	Maximum signal loss that a wireless system can tolerate and still be operational
Message Authentication Code	MAC	Message tag created from plaintext using a **MAC algorithm** and symmetric key that ensures **authentication** and data **integrity**. Common algorithms are HMAC-MD5, HMAC-SHA-1 and HMAC-SHA-512
Message Digest		Output value of a **hash function**
Microcontroller	MCU	Single-chip computer containing one or more processor cores along with on-chip memory and programmable input/output peripherals
Mobile Equipment	ME	The physical **UE** consisting of one of more **MT** and one or more **TE**.
Mobile network operator, mobile virtual network operator	MNO, MVNO	Wireless communications services provider
Mobile Termination	MT	A component of the **Mobile Equipment (ME)** performing functions specific to management of the radio interface. The radio interface

		between **TE** and MT uses the **AT command** set.
Modem (=modulator-demodulator)		Hardware subsystem to convert digital data into a specific format for analog transmission
Message Queueing Telemetry Transport	MQTT	**TCP/IP** Application Layer lightweight, publish-subscribe network protocol
National Institute of Standards and Technology	NIST	Physical science lab and US federal agency responsible for technical administration and standardization
Narrowband IoT	NB-IoT	Cellular LPWAN technology based on **3GPP** LTE standard
Near-field communication	NFC	A protocol for short-range and low-speed communication of two electronic devices over a distance of 4 cm or less. NFC devices can be used for identity or payment tokens.
Non-access Stratum	NAS	In telecom protocol stacks, the highest stratum of the control plane between the core network and **UE**. The NAS layer is used to manage the establishment of communication sessions and for maintaining communications with the UE as it moves.
One-time programmable memory	OTP	Read-only, not-updatable memory which can be written only once
Packet Data Protocol	PDP	Packet transfer protocol used in wireless **3GPP** networks

		supporting packet-switching method (incl. NB-IoT, LTE-M). Contrary to circuit-switched method. When data has to be transmitted, it is broken down into similar structures of data before transmission, called packets, which are reassembled once they reach their destination
Paging Time Window	PTW	period of time during which the **User Equipment (UE)** attempts to receive a paging message.
Plaintext		Original unencrypted data, also called cleartext, i.e., before is becomes **cyphertext** via **encryption**
Platform Security Architecture	PSA	IoT security scheme originated from company Arm Holding
Private Key		In symmetric cryptography, the private key is equivalent with the secret key (shared key). In asymmetric cryptography, the private key is the secret half of the public/private key pair.
Printed Circuit Board	PCB	Sandwich-structured board for assembly and interconnection of electronic components
Point-to-Point Protocol	PPP	A low-level data link layer communication protocol between two systems.
Public Land Mobile Network	PLMN	Unique ID for a network service provider containing country code (MCC) and network code (MNC)

Public-key certificate		Electronic document used to prove the ownership of a public key. For this purpose, typically, a **digital signature** of a **Certification Authority (CA)** is used as a trust anchor
Public Key Infrastructure	PKI	A complete set of roles, policies, and procedures needed to create manage, distribute, use, store, and revoke digital certificates for cryptographic keys and manage a public-key cryptosystem
Power Save Mode	PSM	**LTE** feature allowing **modems** and IoT devices to enter idle mode and lowest power consumption level
Public-key cryptography	PK crypto	Asymmetric cryptographic system that uses a pair of keys (a public and a private key), one for the encryption of plaintext and the other for decryption of ciphertext
Radio Access Technology	RAT	connection method for a radio-based communication network, e.g., LTE, Bluetooth, WiFi
Random Access	RA	Cellular network procedure initiated by user device to apply for data transfer
Radio Ressource Control	RRC	Cellular network protocol used between a **UE** and Base Station incl. connection establishment and release functions. States are differentiating between idle

		mode (RRC_Idle) and active mode (RRC_Connected).
Raspberry Pi	RasPi	A popular single-board computer used for embedded system educational projects prototyping
Real-Time Clock	RTC	Electronic circuit (integrated in a **MCU**) providing exact data and time
Rivest-Shamir-Adleman	RSA	Algorithm used for **public-key cryptography**
Reference Signal Received Power	RSRP	Measured value of received power of the LTE reference signals
Reference Signal Received Quality	RSRQ	Measured value of received quality of the LTE reference signals
Registration Authority	RA	Trusted authority of a **PKI** which is verifying a **certificate** request and defines its content
Resource Block	RB	The smallest unit of network resources that can be allocated to a user
Root of Trust	RoT	Hardware-based secure foundation of a cryptosystem offering ultimate tamper resistance for a **Chain of Trust** used for device **authentication**, secure data transmission, secure boot, etc.
Secret Key		A shared key used for encryption and decryption in **symmetric cryptography**.
Secure Element		A **tamper-resistant** component used to securely store sensitive

		data, keys, and to execute cryptographic functions and secure services.
Secure Hash Algorithm	SHA	A **hash** algorithm that creates a *unique* value for each input.
Session Key		A key used only valid during a single communication session between two parties
Short Message Service	SMS	Text messaging service of cellular networks
SigFox		Proprietary, non-cellular **LPWAN** technology, in unlicensed spectrum
Signal to Noise Ratio	SNR	Quality indicator for a radio data connection. SNR indicates the level of signal power compared to the level of noise power, often expressed in decibels (dB).
Smart grid		IoT-backed infrastructure to facilitate efficient energy supply, distribution and consumption services.
Smart meter		IoT device for measurement of energy consumption. Part of the **smart grid**.
Subscriber Identification Module	SIM	Smart card provided by a cellular network provider to **authenticate** the user device
Symmetric Cryptography		Cryptographic system that uses the same (secret) key for both the encryption of plaintext and the decryption of ciphertext.
Tamper-evidence		In contrast to **tamper-resistance**, tamper-evident

		devices only detect and indicates tampering attempts (but does not prevent them)
Tamper-resistance		Applied hard- and software methods preventing unauthorized use or access to internal data of a device ("tampering")
Terminal Adapter	TA	A device that connects a **UE** to a communications network. In mobile networks, the terminal adapter is used by the terminal equipment to access the mobile termination using **AT commands**.
Terminal Equipment	TE	Communications equipment at either end of a communications link, used to permit the stations involved to accomplish the mission for which the link was established.
Tracking Code	TAC	unique code used to identify a tracking area within a particular network
Tracking Area Update	TAU	procedure initiated by the **UE** when moving to a new tracking area in the **LTE** system
Transmission Control Protocol	TCP	**TCP/IP** transport layer protocol, provides error-checked data delivery
Transport Layer Security	TLS	Standard secure **TCP/IP** communication protocol creating an encrypted link between a web server and a browser. Its predecessor is

		known as Secure Sockets Layer (SSL).
Trusted Execution Environment	TEE	A TEE is an environment for executing authorized code only – and ignores all other attempts
Trusted Third Party	TTP	A TTP provides services or facilitates interactions for a community. A typical TTP is a **certification authority (CA)** in a **PKI infrastructure (PKI)**
User Datagram Protocol	UDP	Core transport layer protocol of the **Internet Protocol Suite**. Simple and fast, but less reliable than **TCP**.
Vulnerabilities		Weaknesses of an **embedded system**, potentially to be used by **cyberattacks**
User Equipment	UE	Any device used by an end-user to communicate. For cellular networks, the UE consists of the **Mobile Equipment (ME)** and the Universal Integrated Circuit Card (UICC). resp **SIM**
Watchdog Timer		A watchdog timer is a simple countdown timer which is used to reset a **MCU** after a specific interval of time – in order to increase system reliability.
WiFi	WiFi	A family of radio access network protocols based on the IEEE 802.11 family of standards. Commonly used for local area networking of devices and Internet access.

Zigbee		Short-range, low-power radio access communication standard

www.ingramcontent.com/pod-product-compliance
Lightning Source LLC
LaVergne TN
LVHW051739050326
832903LV00023B/1008

IoT Design Briefs

The Internet of Things (IoT) is inspiring the industry but is a complex creature. For each new IoT use case, project owners and developers are facing tons of technical challenges. This book series is addressing various design aspects of IoT ecosystems incl. regularly revised technology updates and competitive comparisons.

About this Book

New cellular LPWA networks like NB-IoT and LTE-M are offering unlimited Internet connectivity for IoT devices and unrivaled reliability for business-critical applications. Cellular network standards are complex, but off-the-shelf building blocks are supporting developers to convert IoT visions into reality - and to benefit seamlessly from LPWAN functional strengths, e.g., from lowest power consumption for battery-driven IoT devices or from deep penetration into buildings or for underground sensing. This book explains how to build a decent CIoT ecosystem in short term.

Last update: Jan 25, 2023 (V1.3)

About the Author

Kersten Heins is a passionate consultant for IoT ecosystems, focusing on endpoint devices and embedded security. After his graduation in Munich/Germany, he spent over 30 years in the industrial computing and semiconductor industry as a design engineer and in various marketing positions.

www.iot-chips.com

ISBN 9798355622442

90000

9 798355 622442